A JOURNEY THROUGH MARRIAGE, MOTHERHOOD, AND MILES OF MINUTIAE

In a collection of candid, hilarious essays, Chattanooga, Tennessee humor columnist and television personality Alison Lebovitz takes us on the ride of her life. *Am I There Yet?* chronicles her travels toward official adulthood, from her engagement, marriage, and budding career (milestones she wrote about for a monthly magazine in Atlanta) to pregnancies and parenthood.

The fun is in the journey, as Lebovitz embraces life's small, awkward moments: Looking for a lunch buddy the first day at her new job. Remediating her reputation as the mother of the preschool "puncher." Discovering that a dinnertime disagreement with her husband has become the topic of conversation in carpool. We've all had those moments—the ones that remind us that no matter how old we get or how far we go, we never quite leave our middle-school selves.

On growing up Jewish in Alabama:

Every Friday night, my siblings and I were forced to recite Hebrew prayers and hang out with our grandparents. While all our friends were at high school football games, we were eating brisket and listening to our grandfather belch.

On marriage:

I relish those years when life was just a big game of make-believe. If only weddings were as simple as your best friend marrying your little brother in the backyard.

On pregnancy:

Every night while I watch TV, Alan sits on the couch reading parenting magazines, periodically looking up to offer a comforting, "Honey, you are going to be in so much pain," or, "Do you know how long labor is supposed to last? Good luck!"

On potty training:

The problem is, adults rarely talk to each other about such matters. It's not like I find myself saying to friends, "You know, you had a lot to drink at lunch. I think you should try to go to the bathroom."

AM I THERE YET?

A JOURNEY THROUGH MARRIAGE, MOTHERHOOD, AND MILES OF MINUTIAE

Alison Goldstein Lebovitz

Enjoy the ride!

Alison Lebovitz

⊞ Four Square Publishing

Am I There Yet?
A journey through marriage, motherhood, and miles of minutiae

ISBN: 978-0-9839709-4-1

Library of Congress Control Number: 2011937662

Cover art and illustrations by Cindy Procious
www.cindyprocious.com

Printed in the United States of America
First Edition

Published by

⊞ Four Square Publishing

P.O. Box 4617
Chattanooga, Tennessee 37405

www.alisonlebovitz.com

For Alan, Arthur, Abe, and Levi, who always give me what I need—a great story.

CONTENTS

CHAPTER TWO: Baby on Board

CHAPTER THREE: Potholes and Pit Stops

CHAPTER FOUR: Rules of the Road

CHAPTER FIVE: Am I There Yet?

CHAPTER FIVE: Am I There Yet?

In January 1996, at the age of twenty-five, I left a great
job, a close-knit group of friends, and an incredible city—
Chicago—and moved to Atlanta. It would be a new and
exciting chapter of my life. Or so I hoped.

I T WAS UNCHARTED TERRITORY, AND I DIDN'T EXACTLY HAVE A ROAD MAP.
I was unemployed and single, with few prospects in either arena (much to
my parents' dismay), but luckily I was living rent-free with my Uncle Billy and
his family. Almost overnight I had traded bar-hopping and working at the
Japanese Consulate for babysitting and working on my resume. Life was good.

Okay, life wasn't that good, but I had a hunch that it would be great. It would
just take some time.

In the process of finding my perfect job (working for the Coca-Cola
Company during the 1996 Olympics) and my perfect mate (I started dating
my husband, Alan, a few months later), I needed something to keep me busy
(besides answering ads like "Talent Scout Needed" only to learn that "talent
scout" was actually a euphemism for "telemarketer").

As luck would have it, my first cousin's brother-in-law's roommate from
college, Shane, had started one of those free, monthly, music-focused
magazines that you get at the post office or the local pizza place. So under the
guise of interviewing for an ad sales position, I secured a face-to-face meeting
with Shane, during which I spontaneously pitched him what I thought was a
brilliant idea.

"I'm actually not that interested in the sales job," I admitted a few minutes into the interview, "but I would love to write a column for your magazine."

Caught a bit off-guard, Shane said, "Um, okay, well, what do you write about?" *What do I write about?* Hmmm, I hadn't really anticipated that question. But at the time I was an avid *Seinfeld* fan, so my response seemed equally brilliant: "I'm just going to write about my life."

"Your life?" he asked, even more bewildered.

"Yes, my life. I think it's pretty funny and could be potentially entertaining."

He considered the proposal and then said, "Well, we don't just give out columns. You can submit an article, and if we like it, we'll publish it in our local paper. If we like the next one, we may publish that, too. And if we really like them, then we may give you a column and syndicate you across the ten cities where we publish. And only then do you get paid—twenty-five dollars a column." Shane was like the free-tabloid Godfather, making me an offer I couldn't refuse.

In March 1996, my first article was published in *The University Reporter* under the heading "Unconventional Wisdom." The publication was eventually renamed *Insite Magazine*, but "Unconventional Wisdom" would remain a regular column over the next ten years, until *Chattanooga Parent* magazine was founded in 2006 and offered me a more fitting home for my writings.

When I penned that first passage, I had no idea that I would still be writing this column today. And I never could have predicted that it would so fully chronicle my life—from planning the perfect wedding to starting a new career to raising three children, and realizing along the way that no matter my age, I still have nothing to wear.

There are so many things I'd forgotten about over the years and just as many things my husband wishes I would forget. Fortunately, many of them are included in this book. Like our marital showdown over show pillows. Or our summer weekend in New York City with a toddler who refused to remove his ski cap. Or my shock at being listed as a "homemaker" in my university alumni directory. Or my attempt to use child psychology to get our grown dog to sleep through the night.

I was never a good fiction writer, so when people ask, "Did that really happen?" or, "Did you really do that?" after they read one of my columns, my answer is always the same: "Honey, I couldn't make this stuff up if I tried."

And after all this time, I still give Shane credit for taking a chance on me—not only providing a catalyst for sharing my stories, but also giving me the rare opportunity to put my life on record. Because although he never paid me more than twenty-five dollars a column, the experience of writing about this journey has been priceless.

CHAPTER ONE
Merging Traffic

Limited Engagement

L IKE MOST WOMEN, I HAD MY ENTIRE LIFE PLANNED OUT BY THE AGE OF ten. I would become a veterinarian, marry the perfect guy at twenty-two, and have three kids by the time I was thirty—Sabrina, Kelly, and Jill (named after *Charlie's Angels*, of course). My two best friends would have houses on either side of mine, all our kids would be best friends, and our husbands would be doctors and work at the same hospital. It was the picture-perfect plan.

How simple it all seemed from the confines of a friend's bedroom as we mapped out our individual lives together. How easy it was back then to make decisions about issues and events that would one day be so complex. I now look back at those adolescent years and relish the time when life was just a big game of make-believe.

Take marriage, for instance. If only it were so easy to find the right guy to say those "three little words" to you. If only weddings were as simple as your best friend marrying your little brother in the backyard.

My brother and I are both engaged to be married—though not to each other, contrary to popular belief about southerners. In fact, our weddings will be held just four months apart in two separate countries, the United States and Canada. Which means our parents can have nervous breakdowns in two different time zones.

My wedding is less than six months away, and so far, all I have are a date, a ballroom, and a fiancé. According to *Brides* magazine, that means only 137 more things to do before the big day. A little nervous that I may not know all there is to planning a wedding, I went to the bookstore to scout out the wedding section. In case you are interested, there are about a gazillion books on wedding etiquette, all claiming to be "the number-one wedding source in the world." I even checked out what Martha Stewart had to say about planning a wedding, but unless I decide to plant a rose garden in my backyard or somehow learn to sew my own clothes, her suggestions won't be much help.

"Start thinking about the band," my mother suggested to me on the phone last week. So now I'm thinking about the band, and I'm thinking I have absolutely no idea what kind of band to get. Do we want jazzy-funk, rhythm and blues, Big Band, modern, or a combination of them all? And how many jazzy, bluesy, Big Band, funky groups do you know that can play "Hava Nagila"?

The band is actually the least of my concerns. There are the flowers, the invitations, the guest list, and of course the gown to worry about. I learned early on in the game that what I once naïvely referred to as a "wedding dress" is actually called a "bridal gown." And once again, the number of options is countless. Do I want traditional or modern? Strapless or sleeves? Satin or lace? Romantic or sexy? While I have sought advice from various women who have worn everything from vintage varieties to custom-made couture, my favorite story is the one my cousin Amy tells about her own bridal gown.

Amy was not your typical bride, most obviously because she didn't want to deal with all the details a wedding usually entails—like the wedding itself. She didn't even get married in her hometown, agreeing to have the ceremony in her husband's hometown, instead. And while her mother and sister worked tirelessly to address every last detail surrounding the weekend, when they asked for Amy's opinion, her typical response was a nonchalant, "Whatever."

Amy's method for choosing a gown was equally unconventional. Her Uncle Arnie owned a line of bridal gowns in New York City, and just as he had given her mother a dress for her wedding, he insisted on doing the same for Amy. How could she refuse such a generous offer?

"It was actually the easiest time I ever had picking out a dress," Amy recalled. "Uncle Arnie shipped me three options; I picked the one I liked best and shipped the other two back the next day." And when she ignored Uncle Arnie's repeated requests that she choose a matching veil, he brought one on the plane and gave it to her on the day of her wedding. "It was nice, whatever," Amy said. "The truth is, I had a choice between a big wedding and a house, and I chose the house. Call me crazy."

What's crazy is hearing about the women who go from wedding bells to wedding bills, spending modest fortunes so they can have their "dream wedding" and later facing a nightmarish amount of debt. Oprah once dedicated an entire show to women with wedding regret. She recalled her own experience with a former staff member who begged her for a twenty-thousand-dollar loan to finance a storybook wedding. Oprah turned her down, suggesting that the staffer have a ceremony within her means. Instead, the woman got a loan from another source, had her dream wedding, and is now divorced and still paying it off.

I've begun to realize that my dream wedding won't come from a magazine, a talk show, or a world-class wedding guide. My dream wedding has nothing to do with exotic flowers, an amazing band, or even a stunning bridal gown. In fact, I've known since the age of ten the one detail that would make my wedding perfect: marrying the perfect guy.

My fiancé, Alan, is definitely that perfect guy. I know this because no matter what decisions we've had to make, plans we've had to arrange, or dates we've had to secure, Alan has comforted me with those three little words every woman dreams of hearing one day—"Anything you want."

What's in a Name?

MADONNA LOST HERS YEARS AGO, AND NO ONE SEEMED TO CARE. OPRAH still has hers, but you've got to admit, she hardly needs to use it. And what about Cher? I'm not sure she even has one to lose.

I'm talking about their last names, of course. With less than two months left before my wedding, the anticipation of changing my name has become all-consuming. These aren't just my last days as a single woman, but also my final moments as Alison Joye Goldstein.

I always figured I would change my last name when I got married. I just never really considered the repercussions of such a move.

When I was younger, like all little girls, I would doodle the names of prospective bridegrooms in my notebook during class and practice writing my pretend future married name along the margins of my homework papers. One day it was Alison Fields. The next it was Alison Berman. At the age of ten it was easy to gauge my many affections by counting the number of name combinations that would appear in my notebook on a given week. If the last name didn't sound exactly right with Alison, then the relationship was doomed from the start. It was a flawless test.

I wish I could say this name test went only as far as elementary school. Instead, the older I got, the more useful this technique became. After college, still single and looking, I would play the name game with any suitor that came along. My mother was no better; she seemed to play the game more than I did. "Alison Stein," she would say, as soon as I even mentioned having a date. "I like the sound of it." Of course, she liked the sound of any name that implied grandchildren in the near future.

The irony is that while practicing potential names became a ritual for me, I now find the reality of taking on a new name somewhat disconcerting.

Changing my name in elementary school was as easy as erasing my old one with a number 2 pencil. But changing it now—for real—will mean altering all my legal and official records. This includes my social security card, driver's license, tax forms, bank accounts, voter registration card, and, even worse, my magazine subscriptions. I grow weary just thinking about it.

All of a sudden I am faced not only with the prospect of losing my identity and being forever referred to as "Mrs. Alan Lebovitz," but also with spending the rest of my life explaining to people who I really am. A name familiar to my children will seem like an alias to my past acquaintances. I envision myself, like my own mother, on the phone with childhood friends, pleading, "It's

Alison Lebovitz, I mean Goldstein—well, Alison Goldstein Lebovitz, now. From Birmingham. At least I used to be from there. Do you remember me?"

I think about practical things, too, like my diplomas, my birth certificate, and the other documents that will forever be engraved with a name I no longer use. I wonder what will happen when a future employer checks the references for an Alison G. Lebovitz and finds that none exists. I worry that credit card companies will forget their loyal member, Alison J. Goldstein, and start Alison G. Lebovitz off on a whole new slate with a substantially lower credit limit. To think that all those times I was in major debt during college were for nothing.

Recently I began considering the alternatives to changing my name. We could always hyphenate our last names and both be Goldstein-Lebovitz; I just hope our kids won't be too traumatized by the time they reach kindergarten, and that they'll learn how to pronounce and spell their last name by the tenth grade. I knew a couple who actually dropped both their last names and took on a completely new last name together. I suggested this idea to Alan, but unfortunately, he doesn't share my secret longing to be a Kennedy.

Some of my contemporaries have opted to keep their names, either entirely or at least in the workplace. Some of them also have questioned my resolve to take on a man's name and follow in the footsteps of my foremothers. But does adhering to social tradition necessarily mean betraying my feminist instincts? If I have to have some man's name, why not my husband's instead of my father's?

I don't consider the issue a major ethical dilemma. My only concern in taking a new name after marriage is never having considered the alternatives. I don't want to do something because society expects it of me or because someone did it before me, and certainly not because that's what so-called etiquette calls for. But, much like my ten-year-old self doodling signatures along the margins, I want to sign my new name with enthusiasm and pride, knowing that changing it doesn't mean losing my identity, but augmenting the one I have.

After thinking long and hard about this, I have concluded that having a new last name isn't nearly as important to me as making a name for myself. Right now, the performer formerly known as Prince doesn't even have a name, but aside from a few harmless jokes, I don't see that affecting him. As Shakespeare wrote, "What's in a name?" That which we call a Goldstein by any other name would talk as much and laugh as loud.

At least, I hope so.

Compromising Positions

A WISE MAN ONCE SAID THAT COMPROMISE IS THE MORTAR THAT BINDS THE bricks of a healthy relationship. Okay, so I'm a bit skeptical that it was a man who actually said it. Still, I couldn't agree more.

Take my marriage, for instance. When Alan suggested we keep our place a little cleaner, I agreed to hire a housekeeper. When he asked that I try to be more prompt, I agreed to turn my clocks ahead. And when he whined for more home-cooked meals, I agreed to move to his hometown so he could eat at his mother's once a week. That's just the kind of wife I am—compromise, compromise, compromise.

Unfortunately, my latest attempt at compromise proved only partially successful.

Last week Alan came home and announced the unthinkable: "Honey, we're having a dinner party." I love how men say "we" in situations when they really mean "you." Sure, we were having a dinner party, just like we were going to be pregnant someday. Unless we were planning to serve Lucky Charms and low-fat Pop-Tarts, I had a lot of work to do.

Our separate track records in this arena were nothing to boast about. At Alan's last dinner party, he had to ask five of his friends not to eat any turkey so there would be enough food for the other guests. I can only imagine what Emily Post would say about that situation.

Likewise, the only dinner party I ever hosted—if it could be called that—was the time I cooked a meal for fifteen of my college friends to break the fast on Yom Kippur. The problem was, I had to cook the day of the fast, so I couldn't taste anything I was cooking. The noodles were sticky, the bread was stale, and the brownies were so undercooked that we had to eat them out of the pan with a fork. Luckily, I was dealing with people who hadn't eaten for twenty-four hours and were not exactly picky.

As Alan and I began our strategic planning, it was obvious that our methods were worlds apart. Alan had what I can only call the typical male response to planning a social occasion. He insisted that having a dinner party was as easy as throwing some meat on the grill, opening up a family-size bag of chips, and serving on only the finest Chinet.

Right, and if we stashed a keg in the bathtub, it wouldn't be a dinner party. It would be a fraternity party.

I, on the other hand, had the typical female response. I immediately started to make lists. There was the guest list, the food list, the people-to-call list, the things-to-do list, and the all-encompassing miscellaneous list.

I have lists with similar headings and themes strewn across my house. My refrigerator is a virtual list graveyard; there are lists from 1991 still posted on the door, not because I haven't had time to throw them away, but because I haven't had time to complete them. I even keep a pad and pen on my nightstand so I can make a list of all the things I remember to do just as I'm about to fall asleep. (This is my list of things that need to be put on a list.)

Anyway, for this particular dinner party, compromise was at the top of both our lists. I agreed to set the table, plan the menu, buy the groceries, make the appetizers, and prepare the meal. Alan agreed to stop saying, "That's not the way my mom does it."

While I don't question the culinary skills of my mother-in-law, a wonderful cook in her own right, most women will admit to balking when it comes to using the recipes of any mother besides their own. So I called my mom long-distance and wrote down every one of her recipes that required no more than seven ingredients and five steps, scribbling her various sets of directions around the margins of my food list.

The weekend of the dinner party, I was a raving lunatic. I drove to four different groceries, two Targets, and a Pier I all within a three-hour period and a twenty-mile radius. By the time I was done, I had napkins that matched the placemats, three kinds of olive oil, and even those little corn holders shaped like tiny ears of corn. When I actually bought vegetable-shaped napkin rings, I knew I was out of control.

In the end, the dinner party brought with it good news and bad. The good news was that all of the food turned out pretty well, and our guests were duly impressed with the cuisine, right down to my no-crust chocolate pie. The bad news was that, in the process, I had unintentionally broken a cardinal rule: "Thou shalt not cook for thy husband, lest he suspect you can actually cook."

The very next evening, in fact, Alan suggested I try making his favorite dish, squash casserole. Clinging to fond memories of takeout and cold cereal for dinner, I knew there was only one way to preserve the integrity of my cook-free past while maintaining my recent, hard-earned reputation as a competent chef.

I proceeded to prepare a delectable salmon, savory salad, and incredible corn on the cob, along with the most horrendous squash casserole you could ever imagine. I intentionally added four times the amount of bread crumbs the recipe called for. Upon tasting it, Alan got a peculiar look on his face, and I watched as he repeatedly stuck his tongue to the roof of his mouth. He finally said, "Honey, no offense, but this casserole tastes like mortar."

I just smiled and said, "That's not mortar, Honey. That's the taste of compromise."

Working Lunch

AFTER A BRIEF HIATUS FROM THE NINE-TO-FIVE, I HAVE RELINQUISHED my rights as a free agent and gone back to work. And a "free" agent I was. I did freelance work, and considering the pay, it might as well have been for free. On the other hand, I had all the free time I could imagine, the freedom to sleep when and for how long I deemed necessary, and, overall, a worry-free existence.

But this week I gave up my hour-long appointments with Oprah for morning briefings with Katie and Matt. Instead of walking downstairs to find the latest issues of *People* and *Vanity Fair* sitting on my coffee table, I now stumble into my office to find copies of the *New York Times* and *Wall Street Journal* lying on my desk.

Once you've been unemployed for a while, the corporate world is as scary and foreign a place to an adult as kindergarten is to a five-year-old. And the first day back to work is actually much like that first day of school.

The night before my first day, I stayed up until midnight ironing clothes I hadn't seen in months and stressing over what to wear the next morning. As if anyone would really notice.

I arrived at the office fifteen minutes early to impress my boss, fully anticipating that, weeks from now, he would remember this small show of commitment when I began arriving fifteen minutes late.

The best part of a new job, much like a new school year, is getting all new desk supplies—fresh notebooks, tape, scissors, pencils, pens, and markers, which are now called highlighters. But while school desks are simply work spaces, work desks are viewed as extensions of an employee's personality. What desk would be complete without toys, gadgets, pictures, and other knick-knacks to personalize her surroundings?

I'd spent the last month in relentless pursuit of interesting things to put on my desk. A picture of me with my husband was my first thought—indeed, a must-have—but finding the right picture was tricky. It had to be cute and flattering without looking cheesy or too posed. It had to be small enough to be subtle, yet big enough to scream, "Lookie here, y'all, I got myself a man!"

I finally found that perfect shot of me with my honey, and I put it on one side of my computer while my toys were strategically placed on the other. I carefully set my new, carved-wood basketball game, complete with tiny wooden basketball, next to my miniature Coca-Cola vending machine bank that plays music when you open it. (I bought that treasure one night off of the Home Shopping Network.) Unfortunately, I had to leave at home my most valued purchase—a brand-new Mr. Potato Head. It came with everything I had remembered: the big eyes, the cute little hat, the stubby feet, the ears, the nose—everything except the actual head. At first I'd thought I was just overlooking it; I sorted through all the pieces again and even shook the box just in case it was stuck to the packaging. Finally I had to accept the fact that I'd bought a headless Mr. Potato Head. My only solace was knowing that it happened to me and not some poor three-year-old. At least I got over it, after a day or so.

By the time I had stashed my new supplies, arranged my toys, put up my picture, and turned on my computer (for show, of course, since it wasn't like I had any real work to do yet), it was nearly noon. Figuring my boss would want to treat me to lunch my first day on the job, I patiently waited for him to stop by my desk. Instead, he passed my office, flung a hand in the air, and said, "See you later"—and that one gesture crushed any hopes I had of having a semi-social lunch experience.

So I did what any mature, outgoing woman of the nineties would do in this situation—I called my husband. "I thought we'd meet for lunch today, Honey," I suggested casually. He pointed out that our offices were a good twenty minutes apart, but I didn't budge. "I really don't mind driving over there," I said, now a bit desperate. "Well," he offered, "why don't you just go to lunch with your new office friends?"

"Because," I whispered as I hunched behind my desk, "I don't *have* any friends yet. That's why." He laughed and told me to grow up. I hung up the phone and put his picture in my desk drawer.

At least in kindergarten everyone gets to eat together. And they get to take naps, too. What I wouldn't give some days for a nap in the middle of the afternoon.

I did, ultimately, find some people to go to lunch with, and I did, eventually, put my husband's picture back on my desk. My first day of work actually turned out to be quite successful, as far as first days of work go. I didn't spill anything on my boss, I didn't fax anything to the wrong number, and I didn't fall asleep during a meeting and wake up with drool on my lapel. Not that I've ever done that before.

The greatest part, however, was coming home to five messages on my answering machine from people upset that I was no longer so accessible. I would have called them back, except I'm a working woman now and had more important things to do. Like getting a new Mr. Potato Head.

The Universal Major

I T'S THE HOLIDAY SEASON, AGAIN—FOR THOSE OF YOU WHO HAVEN'T GONE to the mall, read a newspaper, or been able to pull yourself away from the *Real World IV* marathon. And whether you celebrate Christmas, Chanukah, or Kwanzaa, I'm sure everyone is thinking the same thing right now: "Thank goodness I'm not in college."

Well, everyone except for those of you who actually *are* in college. Right now you're probably thinking, "The first *Real World* was so much better." But soon you'll be thinking, "Man, I should have gone to Brown. I hear that grades are, like, optional there." That's because you are about to begin the most dreaded two weeks in a college student's life—finals. And right now you're trying to figure out how you're going to read fourteen novels, write three ten-page papers, start and finish a major project, and study for exams, all without missing *Party of Five*. Well, at least you've got your priorities straight.

Of course, you've probably spent the past four months basking in a study-free utopia, at the cost of enduring a seemingly endless, sleepless hell come December. You now strategically prioritize your schedule, planning which morning classes to skip in deference to all-nighters. You've blocked out a twelve-hour period for writing that first ten-page paper—more than an hour per page, which you figure any intelligent being can handle.

During this time, when the end may seem far from sight, allow me to honestly assure you that what you are doing now will help you after you graduate and will, in fact, be instrumental in your future. Art history, chemistry, political science, English, communications, and yes, even philosophy—they'll get you nowhere. Sorry. I'm referring to the universal major you are studying, the skills you're honing for that greatest concentration of all—procrastination.

Think about it. All the "greats" procrastinate. Take Santa Claus, perhaps the most popular figure on earth. The man has all year, 365 days, to deliver millions of presents to children all over the world. And what does he do? Every year it's the same thing—the night before Christmas, the guy's pulling an all-nighter, probably on a sugar rush from all the cookies and cocoa he's downing, racing all over the planet to deliver his presents.

And you know that Mrs. Claus is just following him around the North Pole, yelling, "Dang it, Kris, I told you not to wait 'til the night before. You do this every year, driving me crazy with your last-minute antics."

What Mrs. Claus may not understand is that procrastination isn't a bad habit; it's a life choice. Just ask any seasoned procrastinator, and she'll tell you she "chooses" to procrastinate. "I work better under pressure," insists my sister,

Amanda, a junior at Boston University. "Besides, college is like a great safari—instead of animals, we're hunting for grades. The end result is important, but the real triumph is in recalling what you went through to get there."

She's right, of course. I once literally "took home" my take-home exams, brought three of them all the way from Boston to my home in Alabama, and Fed-Exed them to my professors the day before they were due. And I still tell people about the time during my sophomore year when I stayed up for seventy-two hours, studying for two exams and writing a fifteen-page paper. I then crashed for twenty-four hours straight without even the smallest sign of consciousness; my roommates periodically shoved a mirror under my nose to make sure I was still alive.

Do I remember what the paper was about, how I did on the exams, or even what classes the exams were in? Of course not. I mean, of course I do, Mom and Dad, but that's not the point. The point is, I am not regularly called upon to recount the details of the War of 1812 or conjugate random verbs in French. Instead, the older I get, the more responsibilities I have, the more tasks I must juggle, and therefore—are you seeing where this is going yet?—*the more things I need to put off until tomorrow.*

I still wait to do laundry until I'm down to my final pair of underwear, run the dishwasher only when I am down to my last semi-clean fork, and wash my hair right at that three-day mark, just before it gets noticeably greasy. But that is mere child's play. I also arrive at the airport as final boarding is being called, finish work assignments seconds before my boss blows a gasket, and pull up to the pump just as my car is running out of gas.

True procrastinators are nodding in recognition right now, relating to these stories and ready to offer similar ones of their own. Then there are the slightly compulsive others, who grit their teeth at the mere mention of last-minute details and get squeamish at even the thought of putting off something of any significance. Like my husband, Alan—definitely of the "Mrs. Claus" variety. In fact, he's upstairs right now, laughing at me, because this column is due in just a few hours. "I don't know why you do this every month," I heard him exclaim, as he walked out of sight.

Happy procrastinating to all, and to all a good night!

Talking Shop

AFTER A YEAR AND A HALF OF MARRIAGE, THERE IS STILL NOTHING IN this world I would not do for my husband. There is one thing, however, that nothing in this world can make me do *with* my husband—go shopping.

Let me preface this by stating that I despise shopping, even though I come from a retail family. My mother works in retail, my father works in retail, my father's father was in retail, my mother's uncle was in retail, my great-grandfather was in retail, I even married into a family that's in the shopping center business. Still, I have an incurable, almost irrational intolerance for shopping. Let me add that leisurely browsing in stores like Target and Barnes & Noble don't count, so you can exhale now, ladies. I'm talking about shopping with purpose and a clear mission in mind.

I'm referring to the kind of shopping that sends little children hiding between racks of clothes for fear their mothers will come out swinging pocketbooks full of lead because they no longer fit into a size-8 dress. I'm talking about the kind of exhausting, frustrating shopping that drives grown women to their knees, salespeople to the brink of insanity, and impatient men to those massage chairs in the mall.

The first time I went shopping with my husband, I should have realized the difference in our basic approaches. Comparing a woman's shopping strategy with a man's is like comparing a da Vinci to a paint-by-number. While women browse and search and contemplate and try on, men buy clothes as easily as they order a special off a Chinese menu: "I'll take the Number 34 in khaki, please." You see, men have sizes; women have size ranges. Men will own the same pair of pants in five different colors; women will own the same color pants in five different styles.

I can spend three hours in a department store, try on eighty-five outfits and thirty-one pairs of shoes, and leave with little more than a headache and a craving for chocolate. Alan can breeze through the men's department on the way to the bathroom, buy ten things without ever taking them off the hanger, and wear all of them until he's eighty. Do you ever wonder why the women's department is always on the upper level and the men's is on the first floor? It's so we can spit on them while they're paying for their purchases and we're telling the salesperson, "Thanks, but I COULDN'T EXACTLY FIT MY BUTT INTO ANY OF THOSE OVERSIZED BAND-AIDS YOU CALL SKIRTS."

I go through nothing less than torture to find a single stitch of clothing that fits me reasonably well, while Alan spends fleeting moments buying what I can only define as the adult version of Garanimals. A few years ago, while shopping for something to wear to a friend's wedding—a black-tie affair, no less—I got so fed up that I decided to do the guy thing and bought a used tuxedo. Unfortunately, more men asked me for refills on their water than a space on my dance card, and I haven't worn the thing since.

Alan would never understand why the tuxedo is still in my closet, along with a number of other outfits that I never wear or that are hopelessly out of style. But the "clothes I can't stand" have to hang in my closet to keep the "clothes that don't fit" company. More specifically, they are my "fat" clothes, my "I think I'm fat" clothes, the all-too-few "look how skinny I am" clothes, and the general "please make me look skinnier than I am" clothes.

The other night, Alan and I lay restless in bed as I fretted over what to wear to a work event the next day. Of course, he offered what amounted to useless suggestions, and so finally we retreated to my closet to scope out the scene together. Just the thought of my husband opening my closet door is enough to give me an ulcer, so I had to be desperate to actually invite him in. He browsed through the massive array of clothes he had never seen me wear before, incredulous at the excuses I offered for each one, excuses that supported what I'd been insisting the whole night and, in fact, every morning, noon, and night of every day of my life: *I have nothing to wear.*

And then Alan did the unthinkable. From the sea of black that washed across my closet, he pulled out a bright-orange, three-quarter-sleeved, double-breasted jacket that I bought in a city I can't remember, from a store I can't recall. Unfortunately, what Alan can't seem to forget is the way I swore I would wear it and how convincing I sounded as I modeled it, twirling across the room and offering the infamous "And it's on sale!" line to close the deal.

"What about this?" he asked. "It fits, it's nice, and you haven't worn it in ages … in fact, you've never worn it. What's wrong with it?"

"I can't stand it, that's what," I responded.

"So, why don't you just get rid of it?" he asked. "You should get rid of all these things you never wear," he continued, and before he could finish counting my useless outfits, I kicked him out of my closet.

And now there are two things I will never do with my husband.

My Hershey/Myself

THE BIRTHDAY CARD FROM ALAN WAS THE EXACT SAME SHOEBOX GREETING card, in the same green envelope, that I have received from him for the past two years. It has become our tradition, one I've sworn him to keep for as long as Hallmark keeps recycling ideas as much as the paper they're printed on.

On the outside of the card are three frames, each containing a picture of a frog wearing a birthday hat and sitting on a lily pad. In the first frame, a fly comes into the scene. In the second frame, the frog snatches it with his tongue. And in the third frame, the frog smiles with satisfaction as he lets out a burp. On the inside of the card, the pre-printed inscription reads, "Hope you get just what you want for your birthday this year." For my twenty-sixth birthday I got this card and an engagement ring—just what I wanted. For my twenty-seventh, I got this card and a treadmill—just what he wanted.

But for my twenty-eighth birthday, there were no guessing games and no surprises. I had picked out my present way ahead of time—in fact, long before I had even met Alan. For a year, I had been saying that as soon as we bought a house, I was getting a dog. Now we were set to move into our new home in September, right after my birthday; the timing was impeccable. Although Alan had put up a valiant fight, trying to deter me from getting a dog so soon, wanting to wait until we had lived in the house for a while, saying we should have kids first, and even questioning my resolve with, "Are you *sure* you want a dog? It's a lot of responsibility!" I told him so was he, but I was sure I wanted him, too.

When I read Alan's message in this year's birthday card, I finally understood why he was so nervous about taking this step. He wrote, "Enjoy the dog ... just don't let it become your best friend."

Four days after we moved into our new home, we welcomed the newest, and furriest, member of the Lebovitz household, a chocolate Lab we named Hershey Bean. Besides always knowing I would get a dog, I also knew I would get a female chocolate Lab and that I would name her Hershey. My sister-in-law added the "Bean" for her coffee coloring, and thanks to our living in the South, the double name actually stuck.

After just two months, I can honestly say that Hershey Bean Lebovitz is the smartest, cutest, sweetest, and most incredible dog in the world, and that I have become the most neurotic, worrisome, compulsive, obsessive Jewish mother that ever lived. Every week I find something wrong with her and call the vet. Sometimes I don't even call; I just take the liberty of dropping in for a brief consultation.

I've also discovered that I would much rather give any behavioral problem a medical excuse than attribute it to my poor parenting skills. She bites incessantly? That means she's teething. She wets her crate at night? Must be a urinary tract infection. She doesn't listen when I tell her "come," "down," or "stay"? Sounds like Attention Deficit Disorder to me.

I grew up with a black Lab named Pepper (you might have noticed a pattern of original dog names in my family), who was the most defiant dog the obedience school and the vet had ever seen. He was sweet and fat and wouldn't hurt a flea, but he escaped through every fence we put up, ran through the house like a horse on speed, and made a weekly habit of collecting our neighbor's trash and scattering it across our yard. What was most disturbing about Pepper's incorrigible behavior was the recurring comment we would hear from our friends: "You know, they say a dog is just like its owners." In our case, the similarities were undeniable.

What made it worse was the inevitable comparison to my aunt's black Lab, Rosie, who could do just about everything but her family's taxes—and I'm almost positive that's because she was never taught. Rosie fetched, she heeled, she sat, she stayed, and her family even had to s-p-e-l-l certain words in front of her because she would get too excited when she heard the word w-a-l-k. Unfortunately, she figured out how to spell that, too.

My goal with Hershey Bean was to rival Rosie's perfection and simultaneously end what has become a legacy of ill-behaved dogs in my family. I wanted my dog to be the most obedient, loving, incredibly bright dog in the universe. Like most Jewish mothers, I had pretty low expectations.

Instead, Hershey Bean jumped on everyone, wouldn't sit, refused to stay, ignored me when I said "come," and was basically the epitome of a Pepper until I remembered the adage "A dog is just like its owner." If my dog really is like me, I thought, there's only one way to get this stubborn pooch to obey: food.

So, I started to bribe her. With every command, however trivial, I rewarded her with a snack, a treat, a c-o-o-k-i-e, whatever it took to get her to do what I wanted. Within a week she was sitting, coming, staying, dropping, even fetching the morning newspaper. Now she's a model dog. A model dog who weighs a few pounds more than she should, perhaps, but who follows me around the house, the yard, and especially the kitchen, hanging on my every word, hoping for just one more morsel.

Alan doesn't need to worry—he's still my best friend. But Hershey Bean may well be my soul mate.

Spectator Sport

I JUST GOT BACK FROM MY SECOND MARATHON, AND BOY, AM I TIRED. MY legs hurt, my back aches, I'm still a bit dehydrated, and I could sleep for the next week. I can only imagine how I'd feel if I had actually run the darn thing.

You see, I'm just a marathon fan; my husband is a marathon fanatic. Recently he took on one of the greatest athletic competitions in the world, the Boston Marathon. While this may be the ultimate challenge for runners, I believe it rates second to the challenge of actually watching it.

Trying to see my husband at three different mile markers along a course with one million spectators, with a single subway line transporting them all, had to be one of the greatest challenges of my life. As I said, I'm still exhausted. But the reward was worth the effort.

For those novice or aspiring marathon spectators out there who might feel threatened or intimidated by a large course, let me give you a little insight into my techniques. I'll begin with some advice: marathon watching is a mentally and physically challenging endeavor *that should be done only by professionals.* Even training for this caliber of spectating is a serious undertaking.

First, never go to a major marathon, especially the Boston Marathon, without some prior observing experience. Watching arena or stadium sports does not count. My personal experience has included watching Alan in three triathlons and the Chicago Marathon, each event more challenging than the one before. At the first triathlon, for instance, I concentrated just on watching him and yelling out an occasional "Way to go, Honey!" during transitions. (A camera, pet, or small child can be very disruptive to the novice spectator and is not recommended until at least the second event.)

At the Boston Marathon, I had graduated to the full-on Timberland backpack, complete with both a digital video and a 35 mm camera, and ten other people by my side, including, at one point, my three-year-old niece. Yet I never lost focus.

Likewise, watching for more than one runner at a single event is an acquired talent. In Boston, my crew and I were gauging my husband, his sister, Beth, and her fiancé, Dan—three runners at one time. This takes pre-planning, precision timing, and the perfect marker. For instance, a helium balloon is colorful and has the advantage of height, but it is often distracting to other onlookers and can be unpredictable in windy situations. We opted instead for my father-in-law's neon-pink baseball cap—bright, easily detected, and multi-functional, as it proved a much-needed head covering in the sun.

Also key to this precision timing are your fellow spectators. It is always wise to watch a marathon with those who are of similar watching prowess. In Boston, I was accompanied by several veteran watchers, including a few with prior Boston Marathon experience. They not only kept up with my pace but were able to take the lead at critical points, including the mad dash to Dunkin' Donuts for Diet Coke.

But endurance is perhaps the greatest quality a spectator can have. The waiting, and waiting, and more waiting … I won't sugar-coat this—at times, it's unbearable.

In the early stages of the marathon, the waiting isn't so bad. You talk, you drink a little, maybe you eat a snack. Actually, the worst part is finding a bathroom, and in this case, creative thinking will get you that extra mile. For instance, my sister had to go to the bathroom between miles 16 and 17, and she used the facilities at a hospital along the same block. (This was her first marathon, too. I couldn't have been prouder.)

But after mile 20, the marathon takes on new proportions. The crowds are at their worst, your snacks are exhausted, your feet are tired, and you think, "I am never going to make it to the finish line." This is when you hit that infamous "wall" and where the mental challenge is at its peak. Because even though you've finished three-quarters of the race, those last 6.2 miles can feel like an eternity. And this is when you have to say to yourself, "I can do this. This is what I've been training for. This is what being a spectator is all about."

Because you have to remember the number-one rule of marathon spectating: there are no guarantees. No matter how much you plan or calculate or train, the bottom line is you may not see the runner at every predetermined spot, and he may not spot you at every predetermined location. But once you make it to the end, there's nothing like watching someone you love run across that finish line and stumble toward you, saying, "Put that stupid video camera away, I'm gonna throw up," and knowing you were there to see it happen.

The Boston Marathon is barely behind me, but I'm already back in training. Alan is competing in a six-hour half-Iron Man in just three weeks. And yes, I'll be there. I know, I'm crazy for pushing myself like this, but hey—I was born to watch.

Crank Shaft

I KNOW WHAT A CRITICAL ROLE MODERN TECHNOLOGIES PLAY IN OUR society. I recognize all the positive things they do, like saving lives, bridging gaps between nations, and giving businesspeople access to their voicemail from thirty thousand feet. But I can no longer sit in silence. I can no longer idly watch as these same technologies ruthlessly strip a basic liberty from our children, turning an American pastime into a distant memory.

I am talking, of course, about crank calling.

For those younger readers, crank calling is when you call someone on the phone, pretending to be someone else, and keep them on the line until (a) they swear at you and hang up; (b) you lose it and start laughing; or (c) you're in the midst of making a particularly inappropriate comment and suddenly realize that you've called your grandparents by mistake.

First, they threatened this great childhood tradition with that annoying little *69 feature. Then they brought out the big guns—Caller ID. Both of these turned out to be relatively harmless, since you could always call undetected from your cell phone or by punching *67. But finally they came out with the nuclear option: Caller ID with unidentifiable call blocking and cell phone recognition capabilities. It was then that crank calling started to hitch a ride on the obsolete entertainment highway.

It wasn't until last week, however, that I realized just how serious the repercussions of these technologies had become. I was calling a friend of mine from the car, and as I'm too cheap to use directory assistance, I tried to dial her number from memory. When a strange woman's voice answered, I quickly hung up. A few moments later, my phone rang, and much to my surprise, it was the strange woman again.

"Hello," I said.

"Yes, hello, did you just call me and hang up?"

Stunned and at a loss for words, I could only sit there and search the area for a Candid Camera truck.

"Helloooooo, I asked if you just called me and hung up. Are you there? I hear you breathing."

"Um, I'm not sure," I began. "I just called a wrong number by mistake and hung up when I realized ... "

"Well, that was *my* number. Next time you should acknowledge you have made a mistake and *then* hang up. Got it?" And with that, the strange woman on the other end of the line was gone, along with my dreams for a future replete with crank phone calls.

I hesitate to imagine a world void of crank calling. Have the Jerky Boys taught us nothing? What will young girls do at slumber parties now? And even worse, what will become of teenage stalking?

Oh, come on, who among us cannot recall a fleeting romantic interest that involved calling someone you liked one or two hundred times a week for the sole thrill of hearing him say, "Hello?"—upon which you would hang up the phone, run upstairs to your bedroom, and scrawl into your journal, "Sunday, March 21—He spoke to me!"

Which reminds me of my friend Debby, who at the tender age of fifteen was cruelly stripped of her own crank-calling rights, long before the advent of Caller ID.

Debby's daily ritual involved calling a certain jock she had a crush on and staying on the line as long as she could without whimpering at the mere sound of his teenage voice. And then, one day at school, an incredible thing happened. The jock approached Debby at her locker and asked for a favor. A favor—from Debby! She couldn't believe her ears.

"Sure, anything," she replied.

She then learned that at the same time she was innocently crank calling the jock for her daily dose of "Hello," the jock's little sister was getting her own dose of obscene crank calls from some boys in her class. So the jock's parents had decided to trace their phone calls over a month's period to catch the little rascals. The jock recognized Debby's number and realized she was the "Hello Bandit" and not one of the obscene callers his parents were looking for.

"So, if you wouldn't mind," said the jock, "I'd really appreciate it if you could stop calling my house."

Needless to say, Debby never cranked another soul again.

I think of Debby's grief, of her misfortune, and wonder if it is better to have cranked and lost than never to have cranked at all. I think Debby would say yes. But future generations will never have that option. They will see the telephone merely as a mode of communication rather than a means of unfettered entertainment. And sadly, they will never learn to ask that time-honored question, "Is your refrigerator running?"

To show my support for this well-deserved cause, I am tossing my own Caller ID unit and making my home a crank-friendly environment. Children everywhere can rest assured that there is at least one person out there who cares, who will set aside these modern conveniences to preserve a sacred rite of passage. So crank call all you want, kids. Because I, for one, will not let innovation stand in the way of tradition. If I'm not home, just leave your crank call on my voicemail. I'll listen to it as soon as I get back from playing "Ring and Run" on my neighbors.

CHAPTER TWO

Baby on Board

Crossing Denial

I'VE ALWAYS IMAGINED THE DAY WHEN I WOULD COME HOME, LOOK LOVINGLY into my husband's eyes, and say, "Honey, I'm pregnant." He'd cry, I'd cry, and we would spend the rest of the evening in each other's arms, relishing this incredible moment. What I never imagined is that when I actually told him, his first response would be a firm, "No, you're not."

It took a few hours and a half dozen pregnancy tests to convince him otherwise, but now I think Alan finally believes that we really are going to have a baby.

Almost immediately after finding out that I was pregnant, I realized how truly fortunate we women are to be the childbearing sex—and, more importantly, how fortunate we are that men are not, because a man would never realize he's actually pregnant. Despite showing Alan the blaring pink lines and *x*'s on my multiple positive pregnancy tests and reading him the very detailed directions on each manufacturer's box, he would carefully examine every plastic stick and ask, "Are you SURE you're pregnant?"

This is just one reason why I am against using the phrase "We're pregnant." *We* are not pregnant. I give Alan half credit for the conception, and he will certainly bear half the responsibility for the child's upbringing, but there is no way he can claim half of nine months of living on saltines and falling asleep before *Ally McBeal*.

Don't get me wrong—pregnancy has proven quite a positive, lately. For instance, instead of asking Alan what he wants for dinner, I now ask, "So, what are you cooking for you and your pregnant wife tonight?" And whenever he disagrees with me, I merely retort, "Is that how you talk to the woman who's carrying your child?"

As soon as I found out I was pregnant, I started thinking about all the things I would need to buy—the right clothes, the right furniture, the right books, the right foods. Alan, however, had only one purchase in mind—the right car. In our case, those two wonderful words, "I'm pregnant," provoked that one dreaded response: "minivan."

Although I told him repeatedly and unconditionally that there was no way he was getting my butt into a minivan (no matter how big it got over the next nine months), he was determined to buy one. And during an especially hormonal week, when I definitely wasn't thinking straight, I actually agreed to let him bring one home to test drive.

"It's incredible," my husband said, elated, as we drove to the grocery store.

"It's a whale on wheels," I responded indignantly.

"It's so spacious and comfortable and practical," he argued.

"So is a muumuu, but you won't see me in one of those, either," I countered.

I guess the real problem I have with minivans is the whole image issue. The thought of gaining forty pounds, struggling to breathe after walking up a flight of stairs, and using my belly as a TV tray is bad enough without having to drive to work and cruise around town in a mama-mobile. I think I deserve a little dignity.

It's not so bad right now, since I'm just a few weeks into my second trimester. The nausea has dissipated, my regular clothes still fit, and yet I am already reaping the full benefits of pregnancy. Instead of trying to hide the usual pooch I call a stomach, for instance, I just tell people that I'm starting to show already. When I have boxes or heavy objects to carry at work, one of my male associates will quickly step in to say, "Here, give me that—you're pregnant!" Best of all, I am now entitled to eat whatever and whenever I want, with the right to invoke that cherished defense, "I *am* eating for two, you know."

And my husband finally conceded that the minivan was a little premature for a soon-to-be family of three, even with a dog. I'm not sure what did the trick, but he seemed to change his mind as soon as I told him I was all for the minivan as long as he drove it and I drove his sports car.

So, my SUV is safely parked in the garage, my kitchen is stocked with all the foods I now love—grapefruit, pickles, Oreos, and hot dogs—and my husband is slowly figuring out the right buttons to push, and that none of them is actually attached to my body. Basically, life is good—so good, in fact, that I told my husband the other night that I'm thinking of getting pregnant more often. Wouldn't you know, he did cry, after all.

Great Expectations

AS SOON AS I ANNOUNCED I WAS PREGNANT, MY SISTER-IN-LAW SHOWED UP at my door bearing various books on topics ranging from breast-feeding (we won't go there yet) to the husband's role during pregnancy (still a mystery to us all). A seasoned expert in baby production, she was quick to recommend one book in particular, *What to Expect When You're Expecting.*

While this book has been extremely helpful in preparing me for the emotional and physical changes I have experienced thus far, I must admit it is not entirely comprehensive in scope. Therefore, after just five months of pregnancy, I have taken the liberty of writing a brief addendum to this "pregnant woman's Bible," and I've decided to release an excerpt of this never-before-seen manuscript, below.

What to Really Expect When You're Expecting

By Alison G. Lebovitz

Expect people to rub your belly without warning, permission, or hesitation when you tell them you're pregnant.

Expect to be really annoyed the first thousand times this happens, especially when there's nothing to feel but the regular pooch that you've been trying to lose since your freshman year of college.

Expect your husband to have frequent lapses in judgment and say things like, "Are you showing, or just bloated?"

Expect the salespeople at every shoe store in town to know you by name.

Expect to experience periodic short-term memory loss, forgetting things just moments after you've said or thought them.

Expect the same women who once told you how wonderful and miraculous childbirth is to now share with you every last gruesome and horrible detail of their labor and delivery.

Expect to experience periodic short-term memory loss, forgetting things just moments after you've said or thought them.

Expect your mother to call at least once a day with odd requests like, "Would you please stop calling the baby 'it'?" even though you don't know the sex, and "Put the telephone up to your stomach so I can say hi to my grandchild."

Expect your grandmother to think a nurse-midwife is a character she once saw on *Little House on the Prairie* and to ask if this means you're planning to have the baby in a swimming pool.

Expect to call your younger brother and apologize profusely for the time you accused him of being the only person on earth who had to stop to use the bathroom six times during a two-hour car trip.

Expect to question how you ever wore tight jeans in high school.

Expect to find more crumbs on your shirt after a meal than are left on your plate.

Expect to be more traumatized than usual at the thought of getting into a bathing suit during your vacation.

Expect your husband to actually believe you when you complain that you have nothing to wear.

Expect to blatantly stare at pregnant women in public and ask your husband repeatedly, "Is THAT what I look like?"

Expect to attribute every gas bubble, stomach gurgle, and bodily sensation to the small creature moving inside you.

Expect a phone call from your mother asking you to stop calling the baby a "creature."

Expect to tell your boss you have no idea what you plan to do after the baby comes and would he mind getting out of your office and maybe not breathing down your throat for one damn minute so you can get some work done.

Expect to apologize to your boss a lot for random emotional outbursts due to raging hormones.

Again, this is but a sampling of my work to date. I fully expect this to be part of the book's next edition and will submit it to the editors as soon as possible so I can get started on my next creative project, a movie entitled *E.T.: The Expanding Tummy*.

Weighty Matters

E VERYONE WARNED ME WHAT AN EMOTIONAL TIME PREGNANCY WOULD be. My friends told me I would cry when I heard my baby's heartbeat for the first time—but I didn't. Then they said I would definitely lose it when I saw its image on the ultrasound. But I was too busy directing my husband with the video camera. Finally, at my last doctor's visit, I proved my friends right. Tears streamed down my face and I wept uncontrollably, just as everyone had predicted. And all it took was a step on the scale.

During the first four months of pregnancy, I was loving life. I gained no weight—nada, zero, zip, zilch. And then, all of a sudden, the pounds started pouring on.

I promised myself when I first got pregnant that the weight gain wouldn't bother me. I told myself over and over again that as long as the baby was healthy, it didn't matter how much weight I put on. Of course, that was before I gained twenty pounds in ten weeks.

The problem is not that I've gained that much weight, but that I had *no idea* I had gained that much weight. You see, I have never owned a scale. Instead, I've always depended on the traditional "If the pants don't zip, lose the hips" method of weight maintenance and monitoring. This technique isn't exactly fool-proof when all your pants have an elastic waistband or an expandable belly pouch. Plus, I have been so consumed with my swelling stomach that I'd failed to notice the accompanying thunder thighs and bulging backside.

I asked my doctor if she had any suggestions to help curtail this sudden, and apparently continuous, weight gain. (That was after I made her swear for the third time that I wasn't carrying twins.) She recommended I stop eating after eight o'clock at night, walk more for exercise, and drink at least eight glasses of water a day—all reasonable requests, were I able to go forty-five minutes without eating, walk down the hall without waddling, or drink a glass of water without having to pee thirty seconds later.

I felt a lot better after e-mailing my friend Ayumi, in Japan. She's pregnant, too, and she confided that she, too, had gained a lot of weight and that her doctor was a little concerned. The bad news for me was that the average Japanese woman gains a mere eighteen pounds during pregnancy (versus twenty-five to thirty-five for American women), and that Ayumi had reached that point with only three weeks left to go. The good news was that I didn't live in Japan.

Everyone I talk to offers the same comforting platitude: "You're not fat—you're pregnant." I guess that's better than the stage I was in just a few weeks ago, when people who didn't know I was pregnant just assumed I was fat. Then there are the few clueless men who will ask a woman if she's pregnant without being one hundred percent sure the answer is yes beforehand. I've had a couple of these types come right out and ask me, and I always like to act really offended and ask, "Why, do I look like it?" before finally admitting that they are right.

I must say that my husband has been completely supportive throughout my pregnancy. I don't think I could go to sleep at night without hearing the occasional, "Honey you are HUGE," or "What is with your belly button?" to remind me of his unconditional love. Those sentimental words really help me keep my chins up on a bad day.

I am actually very happy with my body and the shape it's in, even if that shape happens to resemble an amoeba. And with just three months left to go, I've resolved to follow my doctor's advice and be as healthy as I can. Which reminds me—it's almost eight o'clock. I only have fifteen minutes to waddle into the kitchen and eat some of those cookies I just baked. Luckily, the recipe called for a whole cup of water.

Calling the Shots

WITH JUST A FEW WEEKS LEFT TO GO IN MY PREGNANCY, I DECIDED I should probably sign up for some classes that explain what the heck I'm supposed to do once I actually go into labor. Entering the resource center of the hospital, however, was like experiencing a bad flashback from my college days, when I would wait until the last minute to register for classes. When I told the woman at the desk that I needed to sign up for Lamaze, she smiled politely and said, "I'm sorry, but it looks like we're booked solid for your due date."

Well, like any irrational, hormonal pregnant woman, I decided the only logical course of action would be to cry hysterically until she (a) let me into a class or (b) called security. I can only assume the woman anticipated this reaction, because before I could muster a tear, she offered me a viable alternative: two comprehensive classes that rolled seven weeks of Lamaze into six hours. "Sort of like the CliffsNotes version," she added. CliffsNotes? Boy, this really was like college.

In preparation for these classes, Alan started reading the numerous parenting magazines we've managed to accumulate over the course of my pregnancy. Every night he would sit on the couch, and while I watched television, he would periodically look up to offer a comforting, "Honey, you are going to be in so much pain," or "Do you know how long labor is supposed to last? Good luck!"

But it wasn't until we attended our first "birth awareness" class that I began to relish the state of birth obliviousness I had been in for the previous thirty-two weeks.

There we sat in a room with six other expectant moms and their partners, all waiting for our instructor to give us the Disney version of labor and delivery, when the presentation was more like *Alien II*. It suddenly hit me that our society is definitely on the wrong track when it comes to promoting safe sex and abstinence. If we really want to discourage teens from having sex, we need to stop talking about pregnancy and sexually transmitted diseases and start showing them pictures of the childbirth process.

While I have read a few books and visited my share of Internet sites, I don't think I was fully prepared for the reality of the birth experience. It's an especially hard concept to grasp when your own mother has been telling you all your life, "When I went into labor, your father drove me to the hospital, I went to sleep, and when I woke up, you were there!" I know there have been significant medical advances over the past twenty-nine years, but after reviewing the options, I would contend that this now-obsolete "go to sleep and wake up with child" method should be reconsidered.

The closer I get to my due date, the more people I encounter who ask me, "So, are you going to do natural childbirth?" To which I promptly reply, "Yes, naturally I am going to get a shot in my spine so that I am numbed from the waist down."

I'm sure a lot of women see Lamaze and the related birthing classes as an opportunity to bring them closer to their partners and to help foster a positive labor and delivery experience. But when I walked into that classroom, I had only one question on my mind: When do I get the drugs?

Unfortunately, that part of the class didn't come until the tail end of a three-hour session that described the entire birth process in graphic detail. At one point, my husband whispered in my ear, "Honey, I don't think you need any drugs. Come on, you can do it without them," as if this were some sort of tough-man contest I was trying to win. I thanked him for his confidence in my stamina and kindly reminded him that he would be by my side for the entire experience. I think now he's contemplating getting his own epidural.

After attending the birth awareness class, I decided I should start figuring out what to do once the child is born. So I bought a book on child-raising—the CliffsNotes version, of course. I've been reading it for just two days, and I'm already on the chapter entitled, "How to Raise a Teenager."

I just hope the shot hasn't worn off by then.

Labor Negotiations, Part One

THERE ARE THREE THINGS EVERY WOMAN SHOULD KNOW BEFORE SHE gets pregnant:

1. The nine months of pregnancy you always hear about are really ten.
2. Women with big boobs do *not* have more fun.
3. The concept of a due date is a total and complete farce.

I know this last fact, especially, to be true because I spent forty weeks fixated on my due date. Planned my life around my due date. Was convinced that I would have my baby on, if not before, that due date. When I did not, I was devastated. In fact, I was so hostile and emotional after my due date came and went that my husband started referring to the times I had PMS as "the good ol' days."

Five days past my due date, I had been through a full month of the nesting phase, otherwise known as the "Martha Stewart on crack" period. I had arranged in chronological order approximately two thousand loose photographs dating back to 1984 and put them into photo albums, planted eleven different pots of flowers and placed them strategically around the perimeter of my house, and driven to Target no fewer than a hundred and fifty times to buy things I had no idea I needed.

The morning of the day I finally went into labor, my grandfather called and was telling me about the day my mother was born. He said that he and my grandmother had walked two miles home from the picture show that day. "Start walking," he said, "and you'll have that baby." Desperate, I took his advice.

I started at the outlet mall and walked for two hours straight, stopping only at Nine West to contemplate the purchase of yet another pair of shoes. (Note: When a woman can no longer find things to fit her body, she resorts to buying shoes—and lots of them.) I then headed over to the mall across town and waddled around there the entire afternoon. I walked more in ten hours than I had walked in the last ten months. But it paid off.

At five that afternoon, I started to have my first contractions. When Alan got home from work, I calmly told him that I thought I was in labor. I guess I was a little bit too calm, because he replied, "Okay, but you know I have softball tonight."

Assuming he was in a state of denial, I remained calm and said, "Maybe you didn't hear me, Honey. I am having contractions, and they are getting worse. That means I am going to have a baby. Tonight."

"But it's a double-header," he said, as if the birth of his first child might take precedence over one softball game, but definitely not over two. When I brought my bag downstairs and started to call my best friend to see if she could take me to the hospital, he finally got the point.

We didn't actually leave for the hospital until 11:00 p.m., and I spent the first forty-five minutes telling my life story to the labor and delivery nurse. She returned the favor by telling me that I was only a centimeter dilated—the same centimeter I had been dilated for the past three weeks. Since the ultimate goal is to be ten centimeters dilated, I had a long way to go.

Instead of sending me home right away, though, she offered to let me walk around the hospital for an hour to see if that would help the situation. That's when I realized that having a triathlete as a husband is not quite the same as having a triathlete as a labor coach. We didn't walk the halls; we ran. Instead of timing my contractions, Alan timed my laps. He even gave me a high-five for every pregnant woman I lapped. To make matters worse, one of the other nurses suggested that I do squats to help expedite the process. Well, that was all Alan had to hear. While the other husbands were offering their wives words of comfort or gently stroking their backs through the contractions, Alan was critiquing my form: "You're not squatting correctly, Honey," he'd suggest. "You need to bend your knees more. Lower … lower!"

After an hour of this, I couldn't decide if I was ready to bring my baby into this world or take my husband out of it. But when the nurse checked me again and told me I had progressed to three centimeters, I knew Alan should get the credit.

Five hours later, he would also get a son.…

Labor Negotiations, Part Two

W HEN YOU HAVE A BABY, THIS MIRACULOUS THING HAPPENS: YOU SEE someone for the first time in your life, and instantaneously, you're in love. You can't explain it, because you've never felt this way before, but all you know is that you want to kiss and hug this person forever. It's an immediate bond between you and the one you've been waiting to see for the last forty weeks—the anesthesiologist.

His name was Dr. Johnson, a brown-haired fellow of medium build who had a wonderful sense of humor, a caring nature, and most important, an epidural needle. Within minutes of meeting him, it was like my body went numb. Actually, my body *did* go numb, at least from the waist down, after he gave me what I like to call "a dose of happy juice."

"Miserable" would be an understatement for the way I felt before Dr. Johnson came into my life, or at least into my room. For two hours I had stood, sat, walked, and squatted while also writhing in pain. I had tried the techniques I learned in Lamaze class, but when it feels like someone is thrusting a thousand daggers into your belly, it's kind of hard to remember things like when to breathe. All I can remember is yelling at my husband, "I can't find a focal point! Help me find a focal point!"—as if my life depended on staring at an Exit sign for an hour. I also yelled that this child better be a good one, because I was determined to clone him to get the rest. There was no way I was going to go through *this* again.

When the nurse checked me and I was three centimeters dilated, she asked, "Do you think you can walk around for another hour, or would you like to get an epidural?"

Was this some sort of joke? Let's see … should I walk around in pain some more, or get the drugs? That's like asking, "Would you like to climb Mt. Everest in a bikini and high heels, or soak in a champagne bubble bath while your husband feeds you peeled grapes and sings show tunes?" It was a no-brainer.

"Bring in the epidural-man!" I yelled.

That's when I wrongly assumed that the hardest part of having a baby was over. For the pain I'd felt up to this point was only a fraction of the anxiety I would feel once my child was born just a few hours later.

It had taken me almost a year to carry my son and to learn everything I could about childbirth, but in a matter of seconds, I went from informed pregnant woman to ignorant new mommy. I was prepared for a C-section, forceps, and even a vacuum extraction, but I had no clue how to "swaddle," how to change a diaper correctly, or even how to feed my son.

In my prenatal class, the instructor made breast-feeding seem like the most natural instinct a woman can have. In retrospect, I should have known the class was unrealistic when I was told to practice various latching techniques with the stuffed bear I had brought. Within a few hours of my son's birth, I had already deemed myself a failure at breast-feeding. The first time I tried it, he latched on perfectly. The second time, however, I realized that was beginner's luck. It didn't help matters that my husband, mother, father, and a few nurses were taking turns glancing at my bare chest and asking, "How ya doin'?"

"Oh, just fine," I felt like saying. "My baby is going to starve because I have no idea how to do this, he won't stop crying long enough to eat, and wouldn't you know it, my epidural just wore off and BOY am I in pain down there!"

They finally summoned the lactation expert—the *milk therapist*, as she liked to be called. When she came into the room, I could only look up at her in despair and cry, "Help! I suck at breast-feeding!" She looked at me with a coy smile and responded, "No, ma'am. Someone else *doesn't* suck. That's the problem."

I couldn't really blame the baby for not latching on right away. I mean, here he is, all warm and cozy, and then—WHAMMO!—he's yanked out by his head into this freezing place, fingerprinted like some sort of criminal, and then thrust face-first into something twice the circumference of his head as someone says, "Here you go, little guy—breakfast!" I would be a little hesitant, myself.

Fortunately for both of us, my son eventually figured out how to suck, which meant he didn't starve and I didn't have to enroll in one of those twelve-step programs for breast-feeding moms.

Motherhood is already a challenge, but I knew going into this that it wouldn't always be easy, or even painless. I also know that whatever motherhood brings, I can handle it, because I have strength, support, love, and determination. I also have Dr. Johnson's home phone number.

Picture Perfect

FOR MOST PEOPLE, WEEKENDS ARE A GUARANTEED TWO DAYS OF REST AND relaxation, a welcome respite from the usual stress and commotion of the week. But for my siblings and me, weekends were never that predictable. We spent those forty-eight hours cautiously, knowing our Saturday morning ritual of sleeping late, watching Fat Albert and the Road Runner, and eating cereal that would eventually rot our teeth was always in jeopardy. Because one Saturday a year, without fail or advance warning, my mother would wake us at the crack of dawn and call to us like a drill sergeant, "Kids! Get dressed! We're going to Sears!" It was time for another family picture.

Family pictures were painful enough without adding spontaneity to the situation; I lived in constant fear that my mother would catch me on a bad hair day. And since all the women in my family share the curse (despite how many people call it a blessing) of having naturally kinky hair, *every* day was a potentially bad hair day. There is one family picture in particular, taken circa 1989, in which my hair is so big that it looks like a sixth member of the family. To this day, every time I see it I ask my mother, *"How could you let me look like that?"*—as if she were responsible for my refusing to cut my hair for two years because I was determined to grow out some bad bangs.

But recently a strange thing happened. I woke up one Saturday, and as I can only imagine my own mother did so many years ago, I declared, "This is the day my son will have his picture taken." There was no method to my madness; the decision was entirely arbitrary. But when I called the Sears Portrait Studio and heard, "Good morning. Can I book an appointment for you today?" before I even said a word, I knew it was fate.

My appointment was scheduled for 2:00 p.m., but I arrived at the mall a full hour early so I would have ample time to prep our four-month-old, Arthur, for his first formal portrait. I changed his diaper, washed his face, brushed his curly black hair, and put him in a precious, baby-blue outfit, which his father kept calling "the dress." By the time we walked into Sears, however, my perfectly coiffed child was a perfect mess. His hair was tousled, his eyes were bright red from crying, and to make matters worse, he had drool and snot coming out of every crevice. The front of his dress was completely soaked.

This was mostly because at 1:45 p.m., Arthur decided he was morally opposed to sitting in his stroller. I spent the next fifteen minutes carrying him screaming in one arm while pushing his stroller with the other the length of the mall to Sears.

When we finally arrived at the Portrait Studio, which I soon learned was a fancy name for a room with a digital camera operated by a teenage part-time employee, I quickly changed the baby into his "emergency outfit" and placed him on the designated fake lambskin rug. He couldn't sit up by himself, so we propped him against some blocks, which meant every ten seconds I had to reposition him because he kept sliding onto his back.

I finally got him in the perfect pose, and when he seemed stable enough I moved back, positioned myself by the camera, and made as many funny faces and noises as I could until he smiled and cooed and laughed. I was terribly excited and couldn't believe how easy this was until I realized I didn't hear any clicks; the teenager behind the camera hadn't taken a single picture. A bit stupefied and on the verge of maternal rage, I shot her a look, to which she responded, "Okay, is everyone ready?" When I looked back at my son, he was flat on his back again.

One hour, two hundred repositions, and a brief catnap later, we had a total of six shots of my son. I was emotionally drained and physically exhausted, and it took all the strength and patience I could muster to choose just one photo I could live with.

And that's when I realized how much trauma my mother must have gone through all those years to get a single decent picture of the family. I finally understood that her actions on those Saturday mornings weren't spontaneous; they were part of her well-conceived plan to lend this chaotic experience as much order as possible, so we could all get through it quickly and in peace.

I now carry that picture of Arthur with me and flash it like a badge of honor. When other moms see it, they smile and nod their heads in recognition of my accomplishment.

"We're going back for his eight-month picture in a few months," I tell them.

"Good luck," they say.

And I walk on, knowing that I have become the drill sergeant, the cartoon-wrecker, the wild woman who drags her kids to Sears early on a Saturday morning without notice or remorse. I have become my mother. Weekends in the Lebovitz house will never be the same.

A Basic Existence

I USED TO THINK MY LIFE WAS PRETTY COMPLETE. A HUSBAND, A CHILD, a dog, a house in the 'burbs—what more could a gal want? I'll tell you what—TiVo!

When my husband surprised me with TiVo for my birthday a few months ago, it didn't just make my day; it changed my life. Activating TiVo is like meeting your soul mate—someone who's patient, who's willing to repeat things when you've missed them the first time, who knows your likes and dislikes, and whose sole purpose in life is to satisfy you. It's never missing an episode of *The West Wing* just because your dinner guests can't take a hint. It's being able to pause *Sex and the City* at a critical moment when your husband has to ask you something. It's the realization that you may never have to leave your house or interact with another human being again.

And while I am certain that many of my fellow TiVoholics are reading this and nodding their heads, I am also aware that other people are reading this and thinking, "I just don't get what all the fuss is about." Of course, those are probably the same people who still think basic cable rocks and that "burning CDs" is something pyromaniacs do. There is a TiVolution going on, my friends, and I for one hold my remote high and shout, "Hallelujah!"

But I'm also one never to forget my roots. When I think back to my childhood, I get teary-eyed, incredulous that I have come this far.

You see, I was raised in a four-channel household. The knob on our television set—which we had to turn by hand—had thirteen numbers on it, but only four stations came in with any clarity. Although my parents tried to convince us that PBS was a movie channel, and that *The Wonderful World of Disney* really was wonderful, we never bought it. Our only consolation was that after watching every episode of *Little House on the Prairie*, we realized the Ingalls kids had it even worse than we did.

We begged our parents to install cable, but to no avail. When my mother would argue that we watched too much television as it was, we would always respond, "That may be true, but if we're going to watch television anyway, don't you think we should at least have options?" My father said I might have a future as a lawyer, but not as a cable television watcher.

Despite these oppressive surroundings, we knew there was a better world out there, one filled with remote controls and shows other than made-for-TV movies. Since we couldn't watch cable in our own home, my siblings and I resorted to sneaking it at friends' houses whenever we found the chance. While our peers preferred playing outside or hanging out at the mall, we became single-minded cable addicts, always chasing the next quick hit of MTV or one of those commercial-free channels we'd heard so much about. Of course, this made returning home to our four-channel set all the more difficult and depressing. We could only hope that one day our children would have it better than we did.

And now our childhood dreams have become reality. My brother and his wife were among the first to join the TiVolution, and my family and I soon followed in their footsteps. I am sure my sister and her fiancé are not far behind. Despite the odds against us, we have all blossomed into skilled and successful television watchers, surfing four-hundred-channel systems with the best of them.

But not a day goes by that I don't treasure this TiVo turning point. For every "season pass" I request, for every pause of live-action I command, and for every movie I digitally record for future use, I know there is someone out there desperately staring at the blinking numbers on his VCR, wondering how he is going to record even a single episode of his favorite television show. And when I think of him, I just shake my head and say to myself, "It serves you right, Dad!"

"That Age"

I HAVE NEVER BEEN SATISFIED WITH MY AGE. I DON'T KNOW MANY WOMEN who are. It seems no matter how old you are, no matter how many things you have going on in your life, no matter how many times your mother tells you to enjoy being the age you are because you're that age only once, you always long for something greater. You always want to be "that age."

It's the age that always seems just out of reach—the age that all your best friends seem to reach way before you do, and the age you know will turn your life around. The inherent problem with striving to be that age is that once you reach it, it's no longer the age you want to be. It's no longer "that age."

When I was ten, I wanted to be thirteen so I could have a bat mitzvah. When I was thirteen, I couldn't wait to be sixteen and get my driver's license. When I was sixteen, I counted the days until I was eighteen and in college. When I was eighteen, I spent every night wishing I were twenty-one so I could get into all the bars and dance clubs. And when I was twenty-one—I swear this is true—I really wanted to be twenty-five so I could rent a car without any hassle.

But a few weeks ago, I turned thirty, and that's when it hit me: I've finally reached "that age."

Thirty is the perfect age. You're smart about a lot of things but wise enough to know you still have lots to learn. You're self-confident enough to say, "No," when you really don't want to do something, and polite enough to say, "Yes, I'd love to," when you know you should. You're old enough to be called "ma'am" by the bag boy in the grocery store, but young enough to look behind you, because you're sure he's talking to someone else.

When you're thirty, simple definitions change. *Going out* means going to the grocery store to pick up something for dinner. *Pulling an all-nighter* means you haven't slept a wink because the baby has colic. *Raging, unpredictable*, and *wild* no longer refer to the parties you go to—instead, they describe your mood swings.

You watch The Game Show Network and wonder what Richard Dawson is doing these days. You sing your son the theme song to *The Love Boat* because it's the closest thing you know to a lullaby.

You remember Charlie's Angels when they were Farrah, Kate, and Jaclyn instead of Drew, Cameron, and Lucy. You remember when Atari was cool, Ms. Pac-Man was hip, and Game Boy was the guy in your class who always hung out at the arcade. You even remember when *Saturday Night Live* was funny.

Most of all, you've reached the age when you are actually grateful not to be any other age. I certainly don't want to be thirteen again. (Who in their right mind would want to go through puberty a second time?) I wouldn't want to be sixteen again and have to deal with driving my siblings around everywhere. I can't imagine being eighteen again; once is as many times as I need to be a freshman in college. Turning twenty-one was great, but these days I can't even drink a beer without getting sleepy. And I definitely wouldn't want to be twenty-five again. Although the hassle-free car rental was a plus, the hassle of the dating scene was a definite minus.

I'm certainly not wishing I were older. In fact, when I think about the future, I get totally freaked out—like Meg Ryan in *When Harry Met Sally*, when she cried, "And I'm going to be forty … someday." Instead of looking ahead and wishing I were "that age," I now think about the future and can't believe I'm going to be *that age* one day. Because as far off as forty, fifty, or even eighty seems now, I remember that thirty once seemed like an eternity away, too.

So for the time being, I am actually going to enjoy being the age I am. Because just like my mother told me, I will be thirty only once. Of course, what does she know? She's been twenty-nine for as long as I can remember.

Don't Ask, Don't Tell

I CAN ALMOST SET MY CLOCK BY MY HUSBAND'S PHONE CALL. AT approximately 4:00 p.m. every day, the telephone rings and, under the guise of checking up on the baby and me, Alan asks the one question every stay-at-home mom dreads hearing: "So, Honey, what did you do today?"

Alan assumes this is an innocent question. The problem is, although he asks, "What did you do today?" what I hear is, "Since you were home all day, didn't have to go to an office, and had plenty of time to get your life, the baby, and the house in order, what exactly did you manage to accomplish?"

The response I am tempted to give is a sarcastic, "Oh, I just sat on the couch, ate bonbons, and watched *Oprah*," or a defensive, "What do you THINK I did all day?" Instead, I usually limit my answer to a simple, "Nothing." It's the same "nothing" I used to give my parents when I was in high school and they would ask what I did the night before. I now realize it's also the "nothing" my parents once gave me when their bedroom door was locked and I asked what they were doing.

It's not that I don't want to tell Alan what I do all day; I just don't think he can handle the truth. The one time I tried to give him an honest answer to this question, the conversation went something like this:

> *So, Honey, what did you do today?*
> *Oh, I had a great day.*
> *Really? Let me hear about it.*
> *Okay, well, I ran on the treadmill, and I went to the grocery store.*
> *Go on, I'm listening.*
> *Oh, well, maybe you didn't hear me the first time. I said I ran on the treadmill AND I went to the grocery store. Can you believe it?*

Obviously, he could not. He could not believe that a thirty-minute workout and a routine trip to the supermarket now constituted a "great day" in my book.

I'm sure he was wondering what happened to the woman who used to spend twelve hours a day at the office, manage multiple projects at one time, volunteer, run errands, cook dinner, throw parties, and still find time to watch *Sex and the City* every week. I'm not sure what happened to her, either, but in the past eight months that woman still hasn't figured out how to take a shower and blow-dry her hair in the same twenty-four-hour period.

That doesn't mean I'm not ecstatic with my life and the decisions I've made. It just means I have different priorities, responsibilities, and definitions of success than I did eight months ago.

I would explain all of this to Alan, but a day in the life of a stay-at-home mom would probably seem like a lesson in futility to a man. We spend hours washing clothes and doing dishes that are dirty again in a matter of minutes. We compulsively put books back on shelves, games back in boxes, and toys back in chests, and then we watch as they are scattered across every room in the house. We diligently prepare sippy cups of milk, bowls of fresh fruit, and plates of steamed vegetables, only to watch our children feed them to the dog. At the end of every day, we have a hard time remembering exactly what we did, but we know it took us all day to do it.

And then when our loving spouses come home, instead of hearing, "Thanks for going to the grocery store today," we get, "You bought the wrong brand of orange juice again." Instead of, "Thanks for making sure our baby has everything he needs," we hear, "How many times does a person really need to go to Target in one week?"

I spoke to some of the women in my weekly group therapy session—also known as the moms in my playgroup—and they were quick to validate my feelings with their own, similar experiences. They also assured me that when your husband asks what you did all day, he doesn't really expect an honest answer.

He doesn't want to know that you dropped a jar of baby food on the floor, cut your foot, and almost took the dog to the animal emergency clinic because you thought she swallowed a shard of glass. He doesn't want to hear that you looked online and found that stroller you've been wanting to buy, at half price, only it's in leopard print. And he certainly isn't interested in how you spent half your day trying to decide what to cook for dinner and the other half trying to figure out how to cook it.

So now Alan and I have a mutual understanding. He's going to stop calling me every afternoon to find out what I've been doing, and I'm going to start buying him the right brand of orange juice. Which reminds me, I have to buy the ingredients for this great pumpkin soup I saw on *Oprah* last week. Luckily, I need to go to the grocery store, anyway. We're all out of bonbons.

Ferberizing Hershey

IT HAS BEEN NINE LONG MONTHS SINCE ALAN AND I HAVE GOTTEN A full night's sleep. With a new baby in the house, we expected the erratic schedules, the midnight feedings, and the inconsolable crying. We just didn't expect it from our dog.

Ever since we brought our baby boy home from the hospital, our baby girl, a forty-five-pound chocolate Lab named Hershey Bean, has been intolerable. She has torn heads off of stuffed animals, gnawed nipples off of bottles, and turned teethers into chew toys. But all of those minor annoyances pale in comparison to her latest antic—keeping us up at night.

At first it was the middle-of-the-night feedings, when Hershey suddenly decided that 4:00 a.m. was the appropriate time to get up, eat breakfast, and start her day. So we started feeding her at night instead of in the morning. This worked like a charm—for about a week. That's when Hershey stopped crying at 4:00 a.m. and started crying as soon as we put her to bed.

And that's when you learn that no matter how attached your husband has become to the dog, no matter how cool he thinks it is that she can sit and give him "five" on command, no matter how many times he begs you to let the dog sleep in your room, when she howls in the middle of the night, she is *your* dog.

It's also when you are confronted with a sad truth: you're in one of the many stages people go through when they transition from being dog owners to being parents.

Stage One is when you decide to get a dog and you naïvely think, "Raising a puppy will be great training for parenthood!" Stage Two occurs when you find out you're going to have a baby and you insist, "This won't change a thing. My dog will always be a priority." Stage Three happens when the baby is about two months old and the only time you talk to your pet is when you're screaming, "Dog, you better shut up before you wake the baby!" Stage Four is when friends tell you they're thinking of getting a dog and you quickly interject, "Want mine?"

Clearly approaching Stage Four, I decided I needed to dedicate more time to Hershey and work with her to address her issues. After months of trying to cure her erratic sleep problems on my own, I decided to do what any responsible mother would do for her child—I would Ferberize her.

Ferberization refers to the methods of Dr. Richard Ferber, author of the classic *Solve Your Child's Sleep Problems*. Parents swear by Ferber's method to get their babies to sleep, so I simply adjusted it to apply to my dog, instead. In canine terms, it's basically behavior modification. You train your dog to recognize that when she cries or barks at night, you are not going to (1) take her out of the crate; (2) feed her; or (3) play ball with her. Sounds simple enough.

In practice, Ferberization goes something like this:

I put Hershey into her crate preceded by her normal bedtime ritual. Soon Hershey starts to cry. After five minutes, I go back into the room and comfort her to let her know that I am there and have not abandoned her. I feel pretty silly at this point, because the whole time I am talking to her, she's standing up in her crate, wagging her tail and probably thinking, "Okay, whatever, just let me out so we can play ball!" However, I *do not* take her out of the crate or pet her. I stay in the room for only a minute or two.

If she is still awake and crying after ten minutes, I go back into the room for a minute or two to remind her that I still haven't abandoned her, although the idea of abandoning her on a remote farm somewhere is becoming more attractive.

This scenario continues every fifteen minutes until the dog falls asleep or until I shoot her.

I have put the Ferber method into practice for the past week, and I am happy to report that it is finally starting to work. Hershey is limiting her crying to about an hour, and I am going to sleep before midnight every night.

This method has been so successful that I have started applying other parenting techniques to Hershey's training. In fact, she's in time-out right now for eating an entire bowl of candy off the coffee table. I plan to let her out soon, though. We don't want to be late for Kindermusik.

Bad Mom

AFTER JUST SEVENTEEN MONTHS ON THE JOB, I HAVE ALREADY BECOME the kind of parent I always swore I would never be. I've become that parent I used to stare at in restaurants, the one I would shake my head at in the supermarket, the one I would eye with disapproval on airplanes.

It was so easy back then, in my childless world, to presume what kind of parent I would or would not be. How simple it was for me to judge others as they attempted to pacify or discipline their children, and how arrogant I was to arbitrarily decide whether they were doing it right or wrong.

I came to this humbling conclusion only recently, while having dinner with my one-year-old son, Arthur, and our cousins at a local fine-dining establishment, Steak 'n Shake. My first mistake was thinking that I could wait to feed Arthur until an hour after his regular dinnertime. My second mistake was trying to teach him that eating too many crackers before dinner would spoil his appetite. After taking away his fourth ration of saltines while we waited for our food, I watched with amazement as he went into a ravenous frenzy, crying hysterically for more crackers and then screaming uncontrollably to get out of his high chair. I might have been a novice parent, but I immediately diagnosed this unusual behavior: Arthur was throwing his first tantrum.

A first tantrum may not be considered a milestone in a child's life, but it is certainly an event in a parent's. And while I couldn't have predicted my son's first tantrum, I had been preparing for this moment since before he was born. Based upon my extensive research of tantrums—i.e., watching other people's children throw them—I knew that in this situation I would remain cool and composed, and my goal would be twofold: (1) to teach my son the value of patience; and (2) to show him that tantrums would not be rewarded or tolerated.

Ten minutes later, however, my patience turned into anxiety as Arthur's screaming and tears escalated to a decibel level seemingly beyond human capacity. I could feel the stares of strangers who were wondering, I was sure, what in the world I was doing wrong. I was wondering the same thing myself. I tried reading to Arthur, playing with him, singing to him, even ignoring him, all of which proved unsuccessful in pacifying him. As beads of sweat ran down my brow and my heart started palpitating, I knew I had just one option left—to give the kid whatever he wanted.

Without another moment's hesitation, I lifted my son out of the high chair, at which point the hysterics mysteriously ceased. Then, fearing I was on the brink of TRS (Tantrum Recurrence Syndrome), I allowed my son to do the unthinkable—to run amok in a public place. He ran screaming across the length of our booth at least twenty times, bent the window blinds in several places in order to see outside, drank half my Coke and spilled the other half all over the table, and then proceeded to eat as many crackers as he could shove into his little mouth. And I didn't care, because at last I had something better than a disciplined child. I had a happy child.

Of course, now I am *that* mother—the one who lets her son drink Coke and eat only french fries for dinner, the one who lets her child run wild without care or consideration for others, and the one who dumps discipline for a decent dinner at the first sign of trouble. Worse, I am forced to compete with those mothers who turned out the way I always thought I would, like my friend Christina, whose two-year-old daughter asks, "May I please be excused from the table?" when she's finished with her meal. When my son wants to be excused, he throws his leftovers to the dog and yells, "Done!" while prying himself loose from his high chair.

Well, I may not be the kind of disciplinarian I thought I would be, but at least I'm the kind of mother I always hoped I would become. And while I may not have taught my son any valuable lessons that evening, he certainly taught me a few, like to pick my battles more carefully in the future. This week, for example, my battle is to cut out Coke from my son's diet. Besides, he gets enough caffeine from all the coffee he's been drinking.

The Unhappy Homemaker

W HEN MY NEW NORTHWESTERN ALUMNI DIRECTORY ARRIVED LAST week, I tore open the box and beamed at the sight of my newest treasure. "It's here, it's here!" I shouted, like Steve Martin's character in *The Jerk* when his new phone book is delivered.

Since both my husband and I are Northwestern alumni, I figured our collective years of study and dedication to the school warranted the eighty-dollar investment in a two-thousand-page directory of our peers. Plus, I wanted to make sure my name would actually be in it.

So while Alan made fun of my decision to purchase this pricey purple people-finder, I concentrated on the task at hand: finding my name. I frantically scanned the *L* section and there, in the middle of page 740, was exactly what I was looking for, the listing for **Lebovitz, Alison Goldstein.** But just as I was about to bask in the glory of the moment, I was instead stunned motionless upon reading what followed my entry—the word *homemaker*.

I read the entry again, certain that I had misread it the first time. But after reading it a third, fourth, and eventually thirty-fourth time, I finally realized this was not a typo. It was my life, spelled out in black and white.

A homemaker? Were they serious? This was my occupation? This isn't the fifties, for crying out loud, it's 2002! It says so right on the front of my new Northwestern alumni directory—the same directory, I might add, that all of my fellow graduate students were probably now reading, wondering how the Alison they once knew and respected could have gone from Camille Paglia to Carol Brady overnight.

Four years of college and a master's degree had amply prepared me for a career in anything from politics to public relations. However, nothing in my experience had prepared me for this moment.

What does "homemaker" mean, anyway? Since I couldn't come up with a fair definition of the word, and apparently I *am* one, I decided to look it up. Much to my dismay, I found the following entry: "homemaker: *n*: someone (especially a housewife) who manages a household." Great, so now I was a "housewife," too.

The problem is, I don't know what I want to be called. But I do know that "homemaker" doesn't exactly make my top-ten list. Some would call me a "stay-at-home mom." The problem with that label is that I don't know a single stay-at-home mom who actually stays at home. Like most of the women I know who have chosen motherhood as a full-time career, I am also a full-time community volunteer as well as a part-time "you name it." I serve on multiple committees and nonprofit boards, work on countless fundraisers and annual campaigns, teach a high school seminar, and write this column. Oh yeah, and I take care of a twenty-one-month-old and keep the house in working order while seven months pregnant with my second child.

It's not that I want credit for these undertakings, and I certainly don't get payment for any of them. I just think if anyone is going to give my occupation a label, it should at least make sense.

In order to make room for my new directory before it arrived, I had cleared off one of my shelves and, ironically, come across one of my old book club selections, Ann Crittenden's *The Price of Motherhood: Why the Most Important Job in the World Is Still the Least Valued*. Besides being an insightful and compelling analysis of motherhood from a sociological, historic, and economic perspective (and a must-read for moms everywhere), it also gives the job of motherhood credibility, respect, and merit—things that don't immediately come to mind upon seeing the word *homemaker* next to your name in an alumni directory.

This book has given me the courage to write the Northwestern Alumni Association and alert them to this blatant mislabeling so they might avoid similar errors in the future. In fact, I am sending them a list of substitute career titles that I would find acceptable in future directory entries. These include Chief Operating Officer of the Lebovitz Family, Director of Early Childhood Development, HR (Household Resources) Manager, and Wonder Woman.

In the meantime, I have torn page 740 out of my Northwestern alumni directory and am using it as a dust rag around the house. I figure that's just what any good homemaker would do.

Chapter Three

Potholes and Pit Stops

Mulligans

AS OUR SON APPROACHES HIS SECOND BIRTHDAY, AND WE APPROACH THE birth of our second child, I can't help feeling that this next phase in my life is really a second chance.

I have spent the past two years trying to figure out how to be a great parent, making all the typical mommy mistakes and first-timer faux pas along the way. And then at dinner a few weeks ago, I had an epiphany.

My son was having one of his rare but never-to-be-forgotten temper tantrums in the middle of a restaurant. My husband was out of town, so I was left solo to drag Arthur screaming from the booth and put him in time-out for thirty seconds so both of us could regain some composure.

In the midst of my counting, I stared at his pitiful face, which was covered with snot and tears, and I knew this episode was somehow my fault. I knew that a more experienced parent would have figured out a way to handle the situation without tears and screaming and counting. That's when it hit me: the reason people have more than one child is because eventually we hope to get this parenting thing right.

It's not that my son has had a terrible upbringing, or that I have been a miserable parent. In fact, I would like to think that Alan and I have done a pretty good job so far, and that Arthur is an amazing kid. But let's face it, who does anything exactly right the first time?

With that in mind, I have decided to spend the remainder of my pregnancy taking notes on some of the beginner's blunders that I have made while parenting our first child, and that I hope somehow to rectify with our second. In no particular order, these are just a few of the challenges I face:

Limiting tantrums. I have observed that there is a direct correlation between the number of times you say "No" to a child and the number of tantrums, crying fits, and public demonstrations the child exhibits. To remedy this with our second child, I have decided to eliminate the word *no* entirely from my vocabulary. Instead, I plan to use phrases like "Ain't gonna happen" to convey the same thought but elicit a more favorable response.

Cutting down on housework. I spend the better part of my week picking up Arthur's toys, games, and books, and every day these efforts seem more fruitless as I watch him destroy a room and all its contents in a matter of seconds. So with the next child, I have decided to establish clean-free zones in my house—rooms without bookshelves, toy chests, or even trash cans, where everything is always on the floor and nothing is ever put away. This way, I won't have to spend hours cleaning the same rooms ad nauseam, and my child won't have to waste energy on the "search and destroy" part of his playtime.

Eating in peace. A high chair is to a pleasant dining experience as a car seat is to a safe driving experience—in both cases, it's impossible to expect the latter without the former. Our first child decided to give up his high chair at eighteen months. Since that time, my husband and I have lost all control at mealtimes. To remedy this problem, we have decided to enforce the following rule with our second child: "A child must sit buckled into a high chair at all meals until said child reaches the chair's maximum weight capacity or said child goes to college, whichever comes first."

Learning another lingo. This next goal is simple: to teach our second child a second language, starting at birth. Studies prove that bilingual children have an advantage in the workforce and a greater aptitude for learning additional languages in the future. The bad news is that neither Alan nor I speak any language fluently except English. The good news is that we still have six weeks to learn one.

Taking a time-out. Time-out is a technique used to interrupt an unacceptable behavior by removing the child from the situation in which the misbehavior is occurring. Children stay in the time-out for no more than one minute per year of age. I am not sure who came up with this technique, but I'd like to offer a logical and more effective modification to it. With our second child, I plan to give *myself* the time-out, thereby removing myself from the situation for a full thirty-one minutes, or until the child finds my hiding place.

The more I think about it, the more excited I am to have this second child—a maternal mulligan that gives me the chance to hone my parenting skills. And while Alan and I are certain to face new and unexpected challenges raising two children, I have a fool-proof plan to ensure that our path to perfect parenting will eventually pay off. I just hope Alan wants a really big family.

Basic Training

T HERE ARE CERTAIN THINGS THAT COME NATURALLY TO ME AS A PARENT. How to love my child, how to nurture my child, and how to console my child are just a few that come to mind. But how to potty-train my child? That remains a complete mystery.

I naïvely thought that the transition from diapers to potty would be effortless and natural. I thought that one day my child would wake up and decide that he was done with diapers. I imagined he would spontaneously rip them off his body, grab a Sandra Boynton book off his shelf, and head to the bathroom while declaring, "Be out in a few, Mom." Yeah, right. And one day my husband is going to announce that he wants to do all the cooking and insist that he watch the kids every Sunday morning while I play golf.

What I soon came to realize is that there is a reason they call it potty "training." Much as a coach prepares a novice runner for a marathon, Alan and I have taken on the arduous and painstaking task of training our son to use the potty. Actually, we've replaced the term *potty training* with a new term, *potty bribing*. And I think this method is working pretty well.

There are two things to remember when it comes to potty bribing: timing is everything, and the bribe has to be worth it. When Arthur turned two, I bought him a cute plastic potty that made music when he sat on it. But he soon found other uses for it, such as removing the bowl and using it as a baseball cap. I finally decided that he needed a better incentive to plop down on the pot, so I did what any good mother would do and offered him an M&M to sit on the potty. This tactic proved futile, as Arthur had no desire to go near the toilet, and he had never even seen, much less eaten, an M&M before. Therefore over the next six months I did what any good mother would do next, and started letting my son eat M&Ms. I would whet his appetite so I could bribe him to stop wetting his diaper.

By the time Arthur turned two and a half, the bribe finally worked, and for a single M&M he agreed to at least sit on the toilet. He didn't actually pee, of course, but at least he sat. Over the next few months, and for *three* M&Ms a pop (but unfortunately not a poop), he would sit on the toilet quite regularly. By this time I made sure he performed for his prize, which quickly advanced from three M&Ms to five gummy bears to an entire bag of Buzz Lightyear fruit snacks.

The good news was that after a few months of potty bribing, my son was peeing freely and, more important, for free—he no longer needed a bribe to sit on the pot. The bad news was that he was still what you might call a "midnight pooper," and getting rid of that dusk-to-dawn diaper was a dilemma, indeed.

And then one afternoon, something incredible happened. Just as I had always imagined and hoped, my son woke up from his nap and proclaimed, "Mommy, no more pooping in my diaper." Both shocked and delighted, I beamed at my son and told him how proud I was of him.

"So from now on, where are you going to poop?" I asked, thinking I should capture this moment on video or something.

He proudly responded, "In my underwear!"

This was not the answer I had expected.

"No, not in your *underwear* … " I coaxed. "Where are you going to poop *instead*?"

"On the potty?" he asked, tentatively. That was my cue to unveil my biggest potty bribe to date. I told Arthur that if he pooped consistently on the potty (not that he knows what "consistently" means), he would get a *real* fish and a fishbowl to keep in his room! He was so excited that he agreed on the spot.

Miraculously, for the next three days, he kept his word. He did not poop in his diaper. In fact, he didn't poop anywhere. He had what some experts in the field call "poop-phobia"—the fear of pooping on the potty. And let me tell you, he held that poop for dear life. Every time I suggested he poop on the potty, he refused. He even told me he couldn't poop on the potty because it would make him "sad."

Sad? I felt like telling him it made me sad to think he may be wearing diapers at his bar mitzvah.

Fortunately, after a few days of raisins and pear juice, my son finally let down his guard. It was not on the potty, however. I have now realized that it is going to take a lot more than just the promise of a fish and a fishbowl to persuade my son to drop the diaper. It's going to take time and patience, it's going to take understanding and encouragement, and, most of all, it's going to take the promise of a full-blown aquarium—made entirely of chocolate.

Guys, Girls and Gory Details

OUR BOYS ARE NOT QUITE ONE AND THREE YEARS OLD, BUT I CAN already see how different they are from little girls, especially when it comes to playing. The old clichés about each sex come to life in my basement as I watch Arthur and Abe gravitate toward balls, dinosaurs, and trucks, while the little girls their ages immediately head to the dolls and dress-up clothes that I bought in my attempt to create a gender-neutral playroom. While the boundaries are sometimes blurred, like when my son feels like donning a tutu, or when his female playmate decides to pick up a baseball bat, the likes and interests of boys and girls seem, for the most part, quite different and distinct.

When I think about it, the same holds true for me and my husband—which is exactly why, for one weekend every year, he goes away with the guys and I go away with the girls. These are four days dedicated to doing things with our friends that neither of us would ever want to do with each other. And our trips and experiences could not be more different.

The guys' weekend is a well-balanced mix of sports and gambling. They play a lot of golf, talk a lot of trash, and bet on everything. Every second of every day is planned out, every meal is predetermined, and everything is about beating the other guy at some game. The girls' weekend is the complete opposite. Basically, we pick a nice place to go, start talking the minute we see each other, and stop talking only to eat, drink, or read our books.

On their trip, Alan and his friends walk thirty-six holes of golf a day. On our trip, my girlfriends and I walk thirty-six paces to the beach and stay there all day. The guys are up at 6:00 a.m.; the girls are up by noon. The guys play cards for money; the girls play Scrabble for fun. The guys order room service; the girls make reservations. The guys drink beer; the girls have cosmopolitans. The guys gamble and lose money; the girls shop and spend money.

But it wasn't until Alan returned from his most recent trip that I realized just how different the sexes really are. As he was telling me for the tenth time about this great shot that some guy had on some hole on some amazing course, I interjected to ask, "So, how are the guys doing? How are Jon's kids? Is Steve dating anybody? Is the other Steve moving to Boston?"

He looked at me as if I had just interrupted a critical commentary during the eighteenth hole of the Masters. "They're fine," he replied, and continued with his play-by-play.

But I pressed on. "I hear Steve's been dating a girl for a few months. Did he talk about her any?"

"Yeah, I guess so," he said.

"Well, what's her name?"

"I don't know, Honey," he said, pretty agitated at this point. "We don't discuss those gory details."

Gory details? Since when did a woman's name become a gory detail? Girls not only care about the gory details, we live for the gory details. My friends and I once spent six hours on the beach discussing a guy my friend Rachel had never even been on a date with but had e-mailed a couple of times. We analyzed every word of his e-mails, which she had, of course, committed to memory, and were able to lend some clear insight into the guy's potential as a suitor.

As Alan continued his very detailed account of his golf game, I realized that men do like gory details, as long as they relate to sports. And that my husband wants to discuss other people's relationships about as much as I want to discuss other people's golf games. Guys can spend hours talking about the shot they just made or the one they made the hole before, just as girls can spend hours talking about the relationship they are in or the one they just ended.

That's because no matter how old we are, boys still love playing games, and girls still love playing house. Boys love action; girls love make-believe. Boys love competition; girls love drama. And when it comes down to it, boys need other boys to help complete their games, and girls need other girls to help complete their lives.

My parents were in town last week and brought our oldest, of all things, a set of plastic golf clubs. Alan was ecstatic and immediately took the clubs and our son to the basement, where they played for hours. That night Alan said, "Honey, you should have seen the way Arthur was hitting the ball." I put down my book and turned to listen. This time, I wanted to hear every gory detail.

Hats Off

I CAN STILL REMEMBER THE SPEECH I MADE AT MY BAT MITZVAH. SPECIFICALLY, I remember thanking my parents for their support and encouragement and for always giving me the freedom to choose my own path in life. My exact words were, "As my dad always says, 'You can be any kind of doctor you want.'"

The line might have been sarcastic, but the sentiment was definitely true. While my parents always encouraged me to make my own choices growing up, they also carefully and sometimes not-so-subtly steered me toward the choices they thought were best.

Now that I have two children of my own, I'm suddenly feeling the weight of that autonomy—no longer as a young woman who is becoming an adult, but now as an adult who has become a parent. And even though the boys are still toddlers, I'm already struggling to achieve that delicate balance between giving them the opportunity to make choices and deciding what choices they should make.

In fact, this dilemma came up quite recently, just as my family was leaving for New York City to celebrate our nephew's first birthday. Our three-year-old, Arthur, decided he wanted to wear his baseball cap on the airplane, and he ran inside to get it moments before we pulled out of the driveway. I was thrilled, of course, that he *chose* to wear this particular cap—an Alabama baseball cap that I had bought for him months before, in an attempt to mold him into a die-hard Crimson Tide fan (another *choice* he will have to make).

Imagine my surprise when Arthur emerged from the house wearing not the crimson cap but an old ski hat that he had found in his closet. It was ninety degrees outside, and Arthur was ready for a blizzard, at least from the neck up. He was wearing shorts, a T-shirt, and a bright-red fleece hat that was also two sizes too small. To complete the look, the hat had a Velcro strap under the chin and came to a dramatic point at the top. "Look, Mommy, I found my hat," he said cheerfully.

Not wanting to undermine his *choice*, I decided on a casual approach. "I see that, Honey. Good job," I responded.

But my approach went from casual to concerned as I began to realize the hat was coming with us to New York. During the drive to the airport, Alan and I took turns trying to reason with Arthur; we even encouraged him to leave the hat in the car so it could "rest" while we went on our trip. He wasn't buying it.

Throughout the airport, heads turned to admire our Smurf-like toddler. Every other person would remark, "Isn't he cute," or, "That's a cool hat, little man." Alan and I would smile and then quickly shoot them the evil eye, as if to say, "You're not helping the situation." And on the airplane, every conversation we had with Arthur was pretty much identical to the one before:

> *Do you want to take off your hat?*
> *No.*
> *Do you want to watch a movie on the portable DVD player and take off your hat?*
> *Yes, please. And no.*
> *Why don't we read a book, have a snack, and take off your hat?*
> *No, thank you.*

The good news is that my son is pretty polite. The bad news is that he kept the hat on for fifty-three hours straight, barring the twenty minutes it took to bathe him each night. He even slept with it on.

At our nephew's birthday party, and with our well-insulated son in tow, I finally solicited my family's advice. My mother assured me that this sort of fashion fiasco is common with young children. She told me that my sister used to wear cowboy boots with her smocked dresses. And my uncle quickly reminded me that when his daughter was four years old, she wore the same green dress for three months straight.

After reassuring me that we were doing the right thing by allowing Arthur to explore and make choices for himself, my family also gave me a critical piece of advice: "And when you've had enough of it, just hide the hat."

As fate would have it, a few hours after we returned from New York, the bright-red fleece ski hat mysteriously disappeared. And thankfully, Arthur hasn't asked for it since. Coincidentally, he happened to find his baseball cap that same night and decided to wear it to school the next day.

"That's a great hat, little man," I told him as he got into the car. Arthur smiled, proud of the choice he had made. And I smiled, too, because deep down, I knew I gave him that choice—the choice to wear any Alabama baseball cap he wants.

Mama's Boys

SINCE THE MOMENT MY CHILDREN WERE BORN, I'VE FELT THE PRESSURES of raising people of the opposite sex—of bringing up boys. As a mother, I would imagine the job of raising little women would be somewhat intuitive. I have found the task of raising little men, on the other hand, to be the ultimate challenge.

As a modern woman, I feel it is my duty to raise men with modern sensibilities. I want them to be strong, yet sensitive; courageous, yet compassionate; levelheaded, yet loving. And my husband just wants to make sure that I don't raise a couple of mama's boys.

I don't know who first conceived of the term *mama's boy*, but I'm pretty sure it was a boy and not a mama. What exactly constitutes a mama's boy, anyway? According to Alan, the definition includes (a) any boy who asks for his mommy more times a day than he asks for his daddy; and (b) any boy who freaks out when his daddy tells him that his mommy isn't here right now.

Alan's worst fears were confirmed the other day while he and Arthur were playing outside. During a little rough-housing session, Alan looked at our son and yelled, "WHO'S YOUR DADDY?!" To which Arthur calmly replied, "Mommy." Needless to say, my husband was not amused.

Could it be true? Was his wife raising a mama's boy right under his own roof? While this episode proved shocking and upsetting for Alan, it only verified his longtime suspicions. And that's why, from the moment our second son, Abe, came into this world, Alan was there at every step to ensure he knew exactly who his daddy was.

Of course, the most critical component of being a mama's boy is the widely known fact that this state of being is entirely Mama's fault. It is her fault that the little boy becomes attached to her; it is her fault that he often prefers her to other grown-ups, including his own father; and it is her fault that he seeks her arms for comfort. It's basically her fault that she has the reproductive organs necessary to bear the little boy in the first place.

So while every mama's boy will inevitably suffer the indignity of *being* a mama's boy, he can at least take comfort in knowing he has Mama to blame. And he's not the only one. Daddy will blame Mama as well, and even after the little boy becomes a man and can blame his mother perfectly well on his own, he will no doubt have countless girlfriends, and even a spouse, to help him.

I know this because I grew up with a mama's boy—my own brother. But he's not the classic mama's boy, the pathetic pushover. He's the kind of mama's boy who always knew right from wrong, who always saved his allowance and his Halloween candy, and who always treated women the same way he treated his mama—with respect. Granted, there were some repercussions. He is now a grown man living in New York City, with a great wife and a little boy of his own, yet he still calls our mother on a daily basis to get advice on everything from cooking to clothing. In fact, his wife's favorite story is about the time he needed new khakis and decided there wasn't a store in New York City that carried the right kind. He called his mama in Alabama, and she sent him what was, of course, the perfect pair of pants.

Besides having grown up with a mama's boy, I also happen to be married to one. And even though Alan would fervently deny that label, I mean it as a compliment. Like my brother, my husband is the kind of guy every mother would want as her son. He is strong, yet sensitive; courageous, yet compassionate; levelheaded, yet loving. If that's the real definition of a mama's boy, then my only pressure is to make sure I raise a couple of mama's boys of my own. Just like their daddy.

No Fair

"NO FAIR!" HAS BECOME OUR THREE-YEAR-OLD'S NEWEST MANTRA. Not a day or situation goes by that Alan and I don't hear, "No fair, Mommy!" or "No fair, Daddy!" We must be the cruelest parents on earth. And as simple as this single statement might seem, you'd be surprised at how versatile it can be.

> *No, you cannot eat cookies for breakfast.*
> *No fair!*
> *Please stop feeding your brother sand.*
> *No fair!*
> *The dog is not a ride-on toy, get off her back.*
> *No fair!*

Arthur is relentless, and Alan and I are fatigued. The problem is, there is not much a parent can say to a child when confronted with the age-old, "No fair," except for the age-older, "Life isn't fair." But each time I'm tempted to answer with this reasonable retort, I stop myself and wonder if this is the lesson that I really want to teach our son. And the answer is always a resounding, "I have no idea."

There are universal truths that parents automatically accept and teach their children: You must hold hands while crossing the street. You need to eat your veggies if you want to grow up big and strong. And you're going to do what I say because I said so. I'm just not sure that "Life isn't fair" really fits into that category. On the one hand, I don't want to make our children jaded. On the other hand, I don't want to make them spoiled brats.

So before I could give Arthur a definitive response, I decided to seek out the truth—to find out whether life is, indeed, unfair. After exhaustive study (a Google search), I found that everyone from rabbis to rappers agree not only that life isn't fair, but also that sometimes it's downright wrong. One writer even suggested, "Recognizing this sobering fact can be a very liberating insight … when we don't recognize or admit that life isn't fair, we tend to feel pity for ourselves." So now I was fatigued *and* depressed. And I was late for a meeting.

I serve on the board of directors of a local organization that provides, among other things, a school for children with special needs. Today happened to be our quarterly board meeting, and as I walked into the building, still contemplating my "Is life unfair?" dilemma, my answer quite literally stared me in the face. It was my friend Angel—once a student at the school, and now the receptionist. Physically, she is confined to a wheelchair, but emotionally she is free-spirited and outgoing, always ready with a warm greeting and a welcoming smile.

So I had my answer: life definitely isn't fair. If life were fair, this woman wouldn't have cerebral palsy and be confined to a wheelchair; she would have all the abilities she deserves. But then I looked down at her desk and saw a picture of a beautiful baby girl, her daughter.

"How is she?" I asked, and Angel beamed with delight. "She's absolutely wonderful," she said, as proud as any mother could be.

I knew what she was thinking—that life is wonderful. And suddenly I knew what I was going to say to our son.

I would tell him that fairness isn't a fair way to gauge your life. Life is full of challenges—and equally full of miracles. I would explain that we can't always get what we want, but if we try sometimes, we get what we need. I would tell him that Mick Jagger said that before I did. I would assure him that the choices his father and I are making for him now are going to help mold the choices he will have to make for himself one day. I would remind him that every day he will have to decide whether to point out the injustices in life, or to embrace the opportunities. I would tell him, "That's what life is, Son."

I would tell our son all this, but he is only three years old. So instead, I decided to relay this to him in a way that a three-year-old could understand. The next morning, I let him eat cookies for breakfast.

Potty Language

M Y PARENTS TAUGHT ME THAT USING "POTTY LANGUAGE" WAS NEVER appropriate. But now that Alan and I are the parents of two toddlers, that seems to be the only language we know how to use.

Until now, we've subscribed to the theory that children should be spoken to in a straightforward manner. We have never talked baby talk to our children, we use anatomically correct words when referring to their body parts, and we always try to reason with them using the same rationale we would use with each other. But for some reason, when it comes to the potty, we tend to flush that thinking right down the toilet.

The inherent problem in using adult language with children when referring to the bathroom is that this isn't exactly typical adult conversation. It's not like I ask Alan every hour, "Honey, do you need to relieve yourself?" Or say to my friends, "You know, you had a lot to drink at lunch; I think you should try to go to the bathroom." It just doesn't happen.

On the other hand, any parent will attest to the fact that talking about the bathroom—or the *potty*, rather—can easily consume ninety-five percent of any conversation you have with your children. My friend Andy, a lawyer and the father of two girls, said it has become such an integral part of his vocabulary that recently he stepped out of a deposition to use the restroom and stopped just short of saying, "Excuse me, gentlemen, but I need to go potty."

Every hour of every day, parents around the globe are obsessively asking their children if they need to go or what they need to make, and reminding them to sit on the toilet before doing anything. And believe me, there are at least a thousand ways to convey the same thought.

This is where my husband and I have a parting of ways. Alan, on the one hand, hates the word *pee*. For some reason, he thinks it's disgusting. He will ask, "Do you need to go?" (or, more often, "Can't you hold it?"), but he refuses to integrate *pee* into his potty vernacular.

I, on the other hand, claim that the word *pee* is nothing next to the well-known euphemism *BM*. Ugh, I can hardly write the letters, much less say them. I attribute my deep-seated loathing for that term to the fact that my parents used it incessantly—and often in public—when I was a kid. "Ali, do you need to make a BM?" or, "Honey, try to make a BM. You might feel better." If that isn't just cause for long-term therapy, I'm not sure what is. Can you imagine the humiliation I must have felt? The only thing more humiliating was when my mom made me give my best friend underwear for her tenth birthday. To make matters worse, my friend opened her gifts in front of *everyone*, and

I stood there, bright red, as she held up mine for all to see. I can still hear my mother insisting, "That was a wonderful gift. Everyone can use new panties, Honey."

Alan and I finally decided to come up with a list of acceptable terms for our joint potty vocabulary. In lieu of the word *pee*, I offered up *tee tee*, which he found too feminine, and the lesser-known *pish*, a term my grandmother uses. He rejected both in favor of the more generic *go potty*. We at least agreed that the term *BM* is completely unacceptable, opting instead to use the ever-popular *poop*.

While we are now on the same page when it comes to our own potty language, we do realize there is no way to control the varying verbiage our children may hear or pick up from people outside the home. In fact, we are about to have a much-needed potty talk with my mother. Apparently she told our son she is really proud he has been going tee tee on the potty, and that when he finally makes a BM, she is going to buy him some new panties.

Free to Be Me

ARTHUR, OUR THREE-YEAR-OLD, TOLD ME RECENTLY THAT HIS FAVORITE color is pink. This didn't come as much of a surprise to me, since he was wearing a pink necklace, a pink ring, and a pink tutu at the time.

I have always made a concerted effort to raise our sons with at least some sense of gender neutrality. Nestled among the many trucks, cars, and dinosaurs in the playroom are a variety of dolls, dress-up clothes, and Barbie accessories I have bought to broaden their spectrum of recreational options. My husband suspects this is merely a ploy to drive him crazy, but I insist it is an attempt to give my sons choices that foster their creative expression, self-confidence, and independence. Driving Alan crazy is just a bonus.

It really started a few years ago, when we were visiting some friends who have two daughters. Arthur was intrigued by the frilly frocks the girls would wear around the house and the obvious pleasure they got from parading around in their pinks and pastels. So I decided to buy him his own dress-up box, complete with skirts, gloves, plastic jewelry, a purse, and, of course, the perfect pink tutu. While Alan stared in disbelief as our son gallivanted around the house in his new garb, he remained surprisingly calm and even offered a positive, "Well, he sure does have good balance on those high heels."

I know what some of you are thinking—that I'm subconsciously trying to fill the void of not having a daughter by imposing these girlish rituals on my sons. Oh, please. It's not like I spend afternoons painting their nails and styling their hair (although our boys do have great hair). I just want them to think outside the toy box. I want them to choose the things they play with and the games they play in the same way that I hope, eventually, they will choose their own careers and paths in life.

My resolve was only strengthened when I ran into an acquaintance with her four-year-old son at the mall. As we were talking, her little boy picked up a pair of women's slippers and asked if he could try them on. Obviously embarrassed, his mother snatched the slippers from him and said, "Honey, don't be ridiculous. Those shoes are for girls, not for boys. We'll find you something else." I couldn't get over the look of defeat on her son's face. And the irony was that this is the same woman who dressed her son in smocked outfits for three years.

No matter how small or insignificant our actions or words might seem, their impact on our children's perception of themselves and the world around them is substantial. I know—I'm starting to sound like a modern version of *Free to Be You and Me.* That's because I love that album. Who wouldn't love a soundtrack with football great Rosie Greer singing "It's All Right to Cry"? I probably listened to that record a hundred times a day when I was a kid. It's all about embracing equality and eliminating stereotypes and this little boy named William who just wants a doll for his birthday. And now when I listen to the CD with my own children, I realize that what people like Marlo Thomas and Alan Alda were trying to achieve with this album in the seventies is actually something we have yet to achieve today—raising children without preconceived notions of what is "male" or "female" in terms of occupations, abilities, or even ideas.

If we are going to break down some of these gender barriers in society, we must start the process at home. I know I can't change the world, or even my friend at the mall, but I can make a difference with my own children and give them the freedom to be themselves. If that means my sons will be parading around in pink tutus, then I'm just thrilled. Besides, it might distract my husband enough that he doesn't notice their new hairdos and nail polish.

Nightmare Scenario

I T WAS 3:00 A.M. AND OUR OLDER SON, ARTHUR, STOOD AT THE FOOT OF OUR bed, weeping. "I had a bad dream," he said between sobs. As he climbed into our bed for the third time that week, I realized that his bad dreams were making my life a nightmare, and I had only myself to blame.

Our boys have always been incredible sleepers. They slept through the night by the time they were eight weeks old, always took three-hour naps in the afternoon, and slept twelve hours every night. Even at three-and-a-half, Arthur would stay in his bed every morning, patiently waiting for me or my husband to come in to start his day. Life was good. And then Alan went out of town for a week, and somehow life made a turn for the worse.

The very first night Alan was away on business, I decided to bring out a new storybook before bedtime—a decision I will forever regret. It was a book by Mercer Mayer, a wonderful children's author. In fact, it was a compilation of three of his stories: *There's a Nightmare in My Closet, There's Something in My Attic,* and *There's an Alligator under My Bed.* The saleswoman at Barnes & Noble told me the book is great for kids who are afraid of monsters or other things at night because it offers a funny approach to such common fears. I was sold.

And even when I brought out the book and started reading about the monsters and nightmares and alligators that lurked under beds and in attics and closets, it never dawned on me that while this might be a clever and effective way to cure such phobias, it might also be a way to plant these fears in the mind of a child who had never had them before.

But Arthur seemed to love the book, especially the story about the alligator under the boy's bed. He made me read that one over and over again. Of course, I might as well have been reading *There's an Alligator under Arthur's Bed,* because from that moment on, that's exactly what he thought. That night, he woke up with his first bad dream. The next morning, I woke up with a new bedmate.

Unfortunately, I wasn't quick enough to associate the new book with my son's newfound fears, which explains why I continued to read it every night after that. By the time Alan returned from his business trip, Arthur was not only having bad dreams, but he was also insisting that I keep his closet light on and the closet door wide open—or refusing to go to sleep at night at all.

To make matters worse, I was eight months pregnant and planning to move our eighteen-month-old, Abe, into Arthur's room before the new baby was born. Alan and I agreed that the sooner we moved the boys into the same room, the better our chances of curing Arthur's monster-phobia and regaining our peaceful lives.

Two days later, we moved the spare crib into Arthur's room, along with all of Abe's clothes, toys, and books. We strategically placed the crib next to the closet door, reminding Arthur that little brothers need total darkness when they go to sleep and that the closet door would have to be shut, with the lights off. Surprisingly, he conceded. That night, as we closed the closet door, turned off the lights, and kissed the boys goodnight, I was certain the nightmare was over. It would be sweet dreams in my house once again.

And that's when we heard it—the screaming from Arthur's room. Except this time it wasn't Arthur screaming, and they weren't screams of fear. They were screams of delight, coming from Abe as he jumped up and down in his crib and yelled at the top of his lungs—for an hour straight. That night, what should have been twelve hours of sleep deteriorated into eight hours, because at six o'clock the next morning the entire house woke up to Abe's joyful screaming once again.

I stumbled into their room, happy at least to see the boys laughing with each other. Arthur smiled from his bed and said, "Mommy, I didn't have a bad dream last night. And there's no monster in my closet anymore, right?"

"Right," I said, sleepy but so very thankful to hear him say those words. And that afternoon, as I secretly stowed the Mayer book on the highest shelf in Arthur's closet, I realized why the monster was no longer in there—because the monster was now sleeping in a crib in Arthur's room.

The Amazing Race

THIS SUMMER I STARTED WATCHING *THE AMAZING RACE*, A REALITY SHOW where twelve pairs of contestants are sent on a global sprint to compete in various challenges around the world. As the weeks go by, those who can't keep up with the quick pace are eliminated from the competition until just one team remains. That team wins a million dollars.

The problem I have with the show is this: What's so "amazing" about two adults traveling around the world together? I don't get it. If they wanted to give these people a real challenge, they should make them fly around the world with a few kids in tow. Now *that* would be a good show.

I can just imagine how the first episode would unfold:

The twelve teams meet host Phil Keoghan in my living room, where he informs them of a few interesting twists in the game. For instance, instead of taking thirty days, the race will be done in just three, and entirely along the East Coast of the United States. Couples will be given a few extra pieces of baggage as well, as each team will be assigned three children under the age of five to travel with. Each team will be provided airline tickets, a diaper bag, and a single box of fruit snacks. Their goal will be to travel from my house to New York and back in a single weekend without losing their minds. And the winner will receive absolutely nothing.

Challenges will include

> convincing a two-year-old to take his shoes off when he goes through security;
>
> convincing a two-year-old to put his shoes back on after going through security;
>
> reconfiguring your seat assignments two minutes before boarding time, when you suddenly realize that no two of your five seats are together;
>
> preventing a four-year-old from kicking the seat in front of him before the passenger whose seat he is kicking turns around and kicks him back;
>
> successfully squeezing an adult and a toddler into an airplane bathroom;
>
> keeping the two older children pacified after they realize that you have a DVD player but no DVDs to play in it;
>
> anticipating the needs of a seven-month-old baby with a penchant for screeching;

convincing a two-year-old that the airplane blanket really is
just as good as Blankie, which you left at home by mistake.

Okay, so maybe it doesn't have the makings for a great reality television show, but indeed, this is the reality of my life. A few weeks ago, Alan and I bravely went where no parents should have to go—on an airplane with our three children. And just when you think traveling is hectic and stressful enough by yourself, you realize it is nothing compared to traveling with your children.

That's because no matter how happy and easygoing your child is normally, for some reason he'll have a total personality change the minute you strap him into his car seat and head for the airport. It's as if children have a sixth sense about flying. They know they can get away with acting up because you are rendered powerless to act at all. It's not like you can threaten a child with, "Stop it right now, or I am going to pull this plane over, do you hear me?" And where do you put a kid in time-out on an airplane, the cockpit?

I used to be one of those people who rolled her eyes when any child was seated within a five-row radius of me. When traveling with my own kids, however, I just pray that we are sitting near an empathetic parent or by someone whose children are acting worse than mine.

Couple the unpredictable nature of children with the unpredictable nature of the airline business, and the only thing you can predict is a lot of screaming, crying, and hair-pulling. And that's just from the adults.

For parents, though, it's all in a day's work. Scenarios like this are just one of a million legs we run in the great race of life. And I'd say that's pretty amazing.

No Sweat

W HEN I LOOK IN THE MIRROR AND SEE THE TOLL THREE PREGNANCIES have taken on my body—the spider veins, stretch marks, and less-than-perky boobs—I realize that there is little I can do short of plastic surgery or laser procedures to correct these imperfections. But when it comes to the forty-five pounds I gained during my most recent pregnancy, hope is just around the corner—literally. That's because around the corner from my house is a brand-new workout facility called Curves. It's a great concept—a women's-only club that allows you to get a complete aerobic and strength-training workout in just thirty minutes.

I am not what you would consider a "workout person." I am athletic in the sense that I like to play sports, but I do not like to work out. Running hurts my knees, I can't stand spin classes, and most important, I don't like to perspire. So when a friend told me that she had joined Curves, loves the workout, and barely breaks a sweat, I had to check it out for myself.

A few weeks ago, I walked into Curves for my initial consultation, and it felt like walking into someone's basement workout room. The place is clean but small and sparse, almost quaint. The entire facility is about half as big as a McDonald's, but the service is twice as fast. It's located at the end of a strip shopping center, so I can park my car, get in the club, and start my workout in under three minutes. The equipment is arranged in a circle, and two full revolutions constitute a full workout. The music is usually some techno version of a Donna Summer song, accompanied by an automated female voice that chimes in every thirty seconds to tell you to change stations or to take your pulse. It's like the reality version of one of those *How to Work Out for Dummies* books. But it's also fast, furious, and totally fabulous.

The best part of Curves, however, is not the actual workout. It's the people I work out with: women. In other words, NO MEN. There are absolutely no men on the premises, except for the occasional guy who walks in by accident, having confused it for the barbershop next door. And the Curves women aren't the typical glam girls that you see in the gym, either. They don't come dressed in spandex to show off their buff bodies and flat stomachs. The only spandex most of these women own is probably in their girdles.

That's because the mean age of the members at my club is around seventy-five. So usually, I'm not just sweatin' to the oldies, I'm sweatin' *with* the oldies. And it's awesome. Besides the fact that these women are incredibly friendly and supportive, there is nothing better for a woman's ego than being the fastest and strongest person at the gym, even if most of the other people need a walker to use the treadmill. On the squat machine there is a sign that reads, "70% of people in nursing homes are there because they can't get off the toilet by themselves, so work it, ladies!" I had no idea that going to the bathroom could be a competitive sport, but I am psyched to know that there is finally one in which I excel.

Of course, some of the women at the club are intimidated by my athletic prowess, like my ability to do an entire thirty-minute workout without having to adjust my teeth. Last week, for instance, one of the instructors said to me, "Boy, are you perky today!" Without hesitation, one of the octogenarians nearby piped in with, "Yeah, that's because she's young!" in a tone that was definitely more accusatory than complimentary. And even though I gave her a friendly smile in response, my eyes were saying, "Bring it on, Grandma!"

It's been three weeks since I joined Curves, and I am happy to report that with the help of their staff, and the support of my senior sisters, I have successfully lost a whopping two pounds. At this rate I should be able to shed those last ten pounds of baby weight in no time, which means I can concentrate full-time on my spider veins, stretch marks, and less-than-perky boobs. I just hope "Grandma" doesn't find out how much we really have in common.

Bag Ladies

WOMEN HAVE A DISTINCT ADVANTAGE OVER MEN WHEN IT COMES TO raising children. That's because we possess certain things that men just don't have—maternal intuition, feminine instincts, and, most of all, handbags.

A handbag is like a mini convenience store made out of leather. It has everything you could possibly need, and it's available twenty-four hours a day. Do you have any idea what a woman can pack in a pocketbook? Of course not. That's because the exact contents of any woman's purse is a mystery, even to her. We have no idea what's in there, but we are certain that one day we will need to use it.

Women spend most of their lives carrying an infinite number of things in their handbags, anticipating the moment when one of these random items might come in handy. In contrast, men carry all things critical to their well-being in their back pockets. This is mainly because men are missing the critical "what if" factor in their brains.

For instance, when my husband goes to the supermarket to pick up a gallon of milk and a loaf of bread, he returns home with a gallon of milk and a loaf of bread. When I go, however, I return with a few dozen bags of groceries, including three gallons of milk and six loaves of bread. My husband calls this "shopping overload." I call it "what if" preparation. What if we unexpectedly have people over for dinner? What if one of the milk cartons mysteriously springs a leak in the car on the way home? What if there is a massive snowstorm and we are stuck in the house for a week? These are all very serious concerns, none of which my husband seems to contemplate.

A handbag is nothing more than a woman's personal "what if" bag. And when a woman becomes a mother, that "what if" bag becomes a diaper bag. Without my many years of training with everything from petite Pappagallo pocketbooks to huge and hefty handbags, I doubt I would have been able to transition to the diaper bag so effortlessly, or fully understand the importance of its contents.

While the "what if" value of the diaper bag is something women easily comprehend, it is a lesson men often learn the hard way. Take my friends Brenda and Steve, for instance. They have a one-year-old son, and last summer they decided to trade places with each other. Brenda, a stay-at-home mom, took on a three-month consulting job, while Steve, a high school teacher and coach, stayed home with the baby. The first week of work, Brenda had an incredible time. The first week staying home with the baby, Steve had an incredible revelation; he told Brenda that he had fixed what he saw as a major flaw in her parenting style.

Apparently, while the baby was napping one afternoon, Steve decided to clean out the diaper bag, and he found things he never imagined belonged there—things like toys, Cheerios, wipes, tissues, spoons, straws, money, a blanket, an umbrella, baby outfits, socks, Neosporin, bandages, plastic bags, an old cell phone, and, of course, diapers. He was horrified. "You had way too much stuff in there," he told Brenda, "so I consolidated and kept only the things we really need—diapers, wipes, and Cheerios." To Steve, it made perfect sense.

Brenda could have explained to Steve the "what ifs" associated with each item. She could have given him multiple examples of times when each thing had come in handy or saved her from a potentially ugly situation. Instead, she decided to let Steve figure this out for himself.

The very next week, while Steve and the baby were at the park, the baby took a fall and his knee started to bleed. Steve had no bandages. Steve took him into the public restroom, where the floor was covered in a foul-smelling pool of water, and the baby decided to play in it. Steve had no extra outfit. Steve picked up the baby, put him in the stroller, and headed home. Four blocks from their house, it started to pour. Steve had no umbrella. After Steve finally got the baby dried, bandaged, changed, and put to bed, he carefully collected every item he had removed from the diaper bag, put it back in its place, and vowed never to question its contents again.

And that's why when you ask a woman how she does it all, she'll usually answer with a simple, "No problem. It's in the bag!"

Bedside Manner

A FRIEND OF MINE SHARED AN INTERESTING FACT WITH ME RECENTLY. SHE read somewhere that the majority of married men with children choose to sleep on the side of the bed that is farther from the door. The implication being that they are farther from their children, and therefore less responsible for their nighttime care.

Since I had no other source to credit this information with other than my friend, who probably heard it from someone like Dr. Phil, I decided to conduct an informal poll of my own to see if this information were indeed true.

What my personal research revealed is astonishing. Not only did it show that ninety percent of men indeed choose the side of the bed farther from the door, but also that one hundred percent of them choose to sleep next to the telephone. "Sleeping next to the phone gives me a sense of power and control," my cousin Robert told me. When I asked why he defers that power and control when it comes to taking care of his kids, he passed the phone to his wife.

One woman responded, "I don't think of it as my husband choosing the side farther from the door, but rather that I choose the side closer to my children."

So I thought to myself, "Do the sides of the bed we choose at night actually represent the sides we choose as parents during the day? Do men consciously choose the side that helps them defer to their wives the responsibility for tending to their children's needs? Do women choose the side that reinforces their role as primary caregivers in the home?"

Robert said the real reason he lets his wife sleep closer to the door is so she can protect him in the event of an intruder.

Despite my extensive polling, I decided my research was not yet complete. So I called my mother.

"I always slept on the side closest to the door until about five years ago," she said. "There's a draft on that side of the bed, and now it's your father's turn to deal with it." My father, of course, took the telephone with him.

My mother also claims that when my siblings and I were little, in the age before baby monitors were invented, she could hear my brother, who slept upstairs, calling for her in the middle of the night when he didn't feel well, and that she could be in his room with medicine and a glass of water before he had time to call for her again.

My final piece of research involved a personal testing of this "bed sides" theory. Did my husband and I really *choose* these sides, even subliminally? And is the responsibility really lighter on the other side of the bed? I needed to know. So, one night I asked Alan to switch sides with me. With a panic-stricken look on his face, he responded, "Huh? Switch sides? Why?" When I assured him it was only for one night, and all in the name of research, he finally agreed.

Just moving those few, seemingly insignificant inches across the bed changed my whole perspective. In a weird and enlightening way, the other side of the bed indeed felt different. By switching sides that night, we had in effect switched roles, and neither of us got a decent night's sleep. I felt far and disconnected from my children, as if an imaginary boundary had been drawn. Alan was restless and uneasy—I assume partly due to his newfound sense of responsibility, but mostly because he was so far from the telephone.

The next morning we agreed never to switch sides again. Because even if there is some truth to this "bed side" manner of sleeping, even if my husband chooses to be on the side farther from the door and I choose to be on the side closer to my children, these are the sides that we like. These are the roles that make us most comfortable.

And through this process I also figured out why men are so determined to sleep next to the telephone. It's so they can still call their mothers in the middle of the night.

Minivan Mama

THEY SAY IT'S THE LITTLE THINGS IN LIFE THAT MAKE YOU HAPPY. I SAY it's the "mini" things. That's because after three kids, two carpools, and countless oaths to the contrary, I am now a bona fide minivan mama. Go ahead, start the taunting, the sighing, and the head shaking. But before you throw stones from your glass SUV, let me assure you that I was once in your place.

It wasn't so long ago that I, too, was an SUV snob. I drove my tank around town like I was ruler of the road, looking down on those minivans like they were the muck of the earth. I liked my height. I loved my space. I basked in the feeling of power. And no one was going to convince me to trade my Suburban for such a sorry substitute. But in hindsight, I was merely suffering from "mini envy."

It all started a few years ago, when my family and I went to Ohio to visit some friends who have four kids. When they picked us up at the airport in their minivan, it was all I could do not to roll my eyes and laugh. But as we started to drive, something strange happened. I got this funny feeling in my stomach and a huge grin across my face. And then, as if seeing a minivan for the first time, I said, "Wow, this is an awesome car."

Honestly, I still don't know what came over me. I can only liken this epiphany to the way a woman might know a man for a long time, might see him as a casual friend, with no potential for a long-lasting relationship—and then suddenly see him in a totally different light and realize she wants to spend the rest of her life with him. Or in this case, the next two hundred thousand miles.

So for the past year, I have been driving my very own mini miracle—in black, of course. (I might have lost my mind, but I still have my dignity.) And just three months after I bought a minivan, my husband had a similar epiphany and traded in his SUV for a minivan, too. I like to say that I drive a minivan and he drives a *mani*van.

I have since become something of a mini-maniac. I often find myself trying to convince friends, family, and even perfect strangers to buy minivans of their own, and lately I have contemplated living in my car. Seriously. Just consider the benefits:

Automatic convenience. My husband will agree that the automatic doors alone are reason to buy this vehicle. It takes only a single trip to the mall in the rain with three kids in tow to truly appreciate this feature. An added bonus: automatic doors increase your children's speed and agility, as you often find yourself yelling, "Hurry, you'd better get out before the door closes!"

Family dinners made easy. Every seat has its own cup holder, so we can eat our meals on the road. And the rubber mats make cleanups a cinch. This means spending more quality time together without countless hours setting and clearing a formal table.

Built-in obedience. While in the minivan, all three of our boys are strapped in with seatbelts at all times, at arms-length distance from each other. This provides a safe, battle-free zone that promotes more dialogue among them and less discipline from me.

My minivan is more than just a mode of transportation; it's a way of life. On any given day, it also doubles as an office, a classroom, a theater, a library, a restaurant, a conference room, or a napping place. (I am still working on a bathroom and a shower.) And as we drive around town, I feel like we are the modern-day Partridge Family, going from one gig to another in our happy little family mobile. Sometimes you can even hear us singing the theme song, "… c'mon get hap-PY!"

But for those of you like my dear friend Carolyn, who is probably reading this, shaking her head in disgust, and thinking, "That will never be me. I will *never* drive a minivan," I encourage you to at least test-drive one and see for yourself. In fact, if you are ever in the neighborhood, you are welcome to borrow mine. Just make sure my kids recline their seats before they go to bed.

Sitting Pretty

T HERE IS NOTHING I LOVE MORE THAN MY CHILDREN, EXCEPT FOR MY children's babysitters. And finding the right babysitter is a tedious and time-consuming job ... when you have your first child. Now that I have three boys ages four, six, and eight, I no longer hire babysitters; I recruit willing parties. Over the past eight years, I've enlisted the help of friends, family members, teachers, neighbors—you name it. No one is off-limits. No idea is too outrageous to consider. There are days I even contemplate paying our postman to watch my kids for a few hours. Hey, he seems like a nice guy, *and* he drives. What more could I ask for?

I started babysitting when I was just twelve years old, which proves that desperate parents have been around for decades. "That's not true," my mother will say when she reads this. "You were very mature for your age." And she would be right, of course. I was so mature that I often determined whether I would babysit for a family by the array of junk food they kept in their pantry. I could endure even the brattiest kids as long as I knew I had a full bag of Doritos waiting for me after they went to bed. Now that I am a parent, I keep no fewer than three bags in my house at any given time.

And when I recall some of the characters my parents tried to pass off as legitimate babysitters for my siblings and me, I can only laugh at the memories and relate to their efforts. The best was when my mom's younger cousin, Stevie, babysat one night. I was only ten years old, but even then I knew to be skeptical. "He's not a *real* babysitter," I told my mom. "There's no way we're staying with *him*!" But after a series of strategic negotiations with her, which resulted in a much later bedtime, two desserts, and Stevie agreeing to let me "do his hair," I eventually conceded.

Since my parents both worked full-time when I was in high school, we went through a lot of babysitters during my teenage years—most of them legit. By that time, my parents had started hiring college-aged drivers, which made sense. There were three of us kids, and we attended three different schools and had multiple after-school activities. Until I turned sixteen and could legally become the family chauffeur, there was no way Mom could get us everywhere we needed to be. I assumed it was her responsibility to take us, because we always called these drivers "mother's helpers." At the time, I never realized how sexist that was. My parents both worked, so why weren't these drivers called "parent's helpers"? I'm reminded of the times when I have to go somewhere and my kids ask, "So, is Daddy going to babysit us?" My response is always a sharp, "Yes, but I prefer to call it *parenting*."

Alan and I now realize that hiring the occasional babysitter is not only critical in helping us maintain our busy schedules; it is critical in helping us maintain our sanity. My sister-in-law refused to leave her firstborn with anyone until he was nine months old, so when she finally agreed to a babysitter, her husband was ecstatic. "Where do you want to go tonight?" he asked. "You name it!" She told him to drive her to the nearest parking lot so she could put her seat back and sleep for a few hours.

As parents, we've all been there—torn between wanting to give our children all our time and energy, and also needing time apart to restore our energy for our children. So, to all the grandparents, cousins, friends, neighbors, teenage sitters, and college-bound drivers who have given all of us parents a chance to run that errand, go on that date, or finally get to that book club meeting, let me just say thank you. You have made our jobs a little easier, our lives a little sweeter, and our roles as parents just a little less challenging.

Which reminds me of my current challenge: to find someone who can babysit on Sunday so Alan and I can go to a movie. Lucky for me, I've got Doritos in the pantry and it's the postman's day off.

Chapter Four

Rules of the Road

Socratic Method

I ALWAYS KNEW THAT STUDYING PHILOSOPHY IN COLLEGE WOULD COME IN handy someday. As it turns out, the Socratic method of teaching has proven quite effective when it comes to parenting.

I would estimate that each of my three children asks me about five thousand questions on a daily basis. And I usually can answer about three of those questions with some degree of certainty. For the others, either I make an educated guess, or I just make things up. "Why are frogs green?" *Because they eat a lot of peas.* "Will I turn green if I eat a lot of peas?" *No, you are not a frog.*

Unfortunately, our children will be this young and naïve for only so long. They will soon realize that I know little about which I speak, and more important, that watermelons will not really grow in your stomach if you swallow the seeds. With this in mind, I have decided to stop faking it and to start using the Socratic method of parenting.

The Socratic method is a conversation wherein two or more people assist one another in finding the answers to difficult questions. In other words, when a child asks you a question you don't know the answer to, all you have to do is ask him a question in return. It's that simple.

Child:	Mommy, how did God create the universe?
Parent:	How do *you* think God created the universe?
Child:	With a huge paintbrush.
Parent:	Very good.

Child:	Mommy, how did the doctor get me out of your tummy?
Parent:	How do *you* think he got you out of my tummy?
Child:	With a magic wand.
Parent:	You are so smart.

There is a distinct philosophical difference between the way parents may use this method and the way Socrates intended it to be used. Socrates developed this type of learning to broaden his students' understanding of the universe and to give them the benefit of true comprehension. Parents, on the other hand, use this method to avoid looking ignorant. By employing this classic technique, they can easily get through years, even decades, of parenting without their child ever realizing how little they truly know.

When I think back to my own childhood, I realize that my father was the original master of this method. In fact, I can't remember a single instance when he answered one of my siblings or me with a direct response. That's probably because every question we asked him was ultimately met with the same question in return—"What did your mother say?"

The good news is that the Socratic method of parenting can safely be used throughout the early stages of childhood development without the child suffering any negative repercussions or ever questioning his parent's omniscience. The bad news is that this method, like any, involves certain limitations. For instance, when a child asks, "Mommy, what's for breakfast?" it is not recommended that you respond with, "What do *you* want for breakfast?" This may result in the child fixing himself a bowl of M&Ms mixed with Cheetos.

This is just a guess, of course.

Finally, this method is not recommended for the pre-teen and later years, or for dealing with controversial topics such as sex, drugs, or Britney Spears. Parents in these situations should instead consider the Descartes method, which promotes the universal truth, "I think, therefore I am." Or, translated into parental terms, "You'll do it because I said so."

The Fight

M Y BEST FRIEND CALLED ME THE OTHER NIGHT AND CASUALLY mentioned hearing about the fight that Alan and I had had the night before. My first reaction was to blame my husband—not only for instigating the so-called fight, but also for blabbing about it, as I was certain he was her source. However, my friend told me she didn't hear about it from my husband. She heard it from our four-year-old son.

Yes, the topic of conversation in carpool that morning was not about the "letter of the week" or even what the kids' moms had packed them for lunch that day. It was about the fight that Arthur's mommy and daddy had had at the dinner table. This was not the kind of PR that I needed in preschool.

In my own defense, let me just say that Alan and I don't fight. We may not always agree on everything, we may quibble, we may get into some heartfelt, passionate discussions, but we don't fight.

Of course, one of the most common arguments we have is over the fact that when we do argue, he never gets to have the last word. That's mainly because I always get to have the last word. Even when he manages somehow to sneak in what he presumes to be the last word, it's really just the first word of a new discussion.

And our disagreements are usually about silly things: the way the dishes have been put in the dishwasher, whose turn it was to feed the dog, why it has taken me all day to *not* bring in the mail. Some of these disagreements do take place over dinner, but our most recent one took place *because* of dinner. This is the "fight" in question.

It all started because I decided to spice up my mealtime repertoire. I am what you would call a "meat and potatoes" cook. I always stick to the basics and to what I know—usually some kind of meat and some kind of potato. But recently, I decided to be bold and break away from the mundane meals. The result was a gastronomical experiment gone bad. The salmon was overcooked, the olive oil for the bread was rancid, the rice was dry, the veggies were mushy … it was so bad that even the dog wouldn't eat the scraps off the floor. Even so, my effort was genuine, which is more than I can say for my husband's; as soon as my back was turned, Alan tried to scrape his full plate into the trash can. I caught him in the act, so shocked and hurt that I almost started to cry. Every woman knows that if she holds back tears long enough, that hurt slowly turns into rage. And a woman's rage is far worse than a woman's tears.

Although I was hurt and mad, I did what any mother would do in front of her three children: I calmly told my husband how upset his actions had made me, and then I took all three kids upstairs to play, leaving him to do the dishes. And that was our "fight."

That's why we needed to explain to Arthur the difference between *arguing* and *fighting*. So the next night at dinner, Alan and I explained that sometimes adults disagree about things, and sometimes they might even argue, but that doesn't mean they fight.

"And you don't need to be telling people what Mommy and I say to each other," Alan added. "What goes on in our house is private."

I gave Alan that look we women tend to give our husbands and said, "Honey, we don't need to tell him what he can and cannot tell other people. The point is to explain to him that it's okay to disagree, but that doesn't mean we fight."

"No," Alan retorted, "the point is, Arthur doesn't need to be telling people things like that, and I think that's the important lesson here."

To which I responded, "Oh, is that a fact?"

And then before Alan and I could say another word, Arthur broke into the conversation and said, "This is what I'm talking about. You're fighting."

Alan and I sat stunned for a moment, shamed into silence. And then we both started laughing, and I knew we were thinking the same thing: for once, someone other than me had gotten the last word.

A Fish Story

THERE ARE CERTAIN LIFE PHASES THAT PARENTS KNOW THEY MUST prepare their children for: loving someone, caring for someone, and, ultimately, losing someone. These are complex, often esoteric concepts—ones that you might spend years trying to convey through careful explanations, thoughtful discussions, and practical experiences.

Or, you could just buy your kid a fish.

In this case, I decided to buy a goldfish for my best friend's daughter. For months, five-year-old Hannah and I had contemplated the virtues of getting her first pet. She would keep it in her room, care for it, feed it, love it, and give it a special name.

My own children have a goldfish already. They know the virtues also include Mommy feeding the fish, Mommy cleaning the tank, Mommy buying a new filter, and Mommy yelling at the dog for eating the fish food again.

Hannah was excited to be a first-time pet owner. Her parents were just thrilled it wasn't a pet they had to walk.

So the day before Hannah's sixth birthday, I went out and bought a marvelous little calico goldfish. Its unique black and orange markings made it impossible to forget and therefore impossible to replace. I had to keep it at my house because her parents were out of town, but the day I got it, Hannah came over to visit her soon-to-be new best friend.

Can you guess the punch line here? The very next day, on Hannah's birthday, no less, ten minutes before I'm supposed to pick up carpool—the fish dies. On my watch! Overnight, I go from the hero who buys a little girl her first pet (which she had already named, by the way) to the woman who now has to explain death to a first-grader. I decided to do what any honest, caring parent would do in my situation: I lied.

When I picked up carpool that afternoon, I started the conversation out on a gentle note. "Hannah," I said, "we need to talk about your fish. I'm afraid he is no longer with us."

"HE DIED?!" my son immediately shouted. "The fish already died?"

"Um, yes," I replied. "I'm afraid so." And then I went into a long dissertation about how I called the pet shop and they explained that even though the fish was really small, it was actually really, really old and had lived a long, long, long life. At least by goldfish standards.

I looked at Hannah, who was looking back at me with a combination of sadness and suspicion. I suppose my fish story sounded a little too fishy.

"So even though the fish was really small, it was really old?" she asked.

Before I could answer, Arthur interjected, "You know, that happens to people, too. Some people get smaller the older they get—like my Nana. She was really old, but she was really short, right Mommy?" Way to back me up, Son.

On the way home from school, we held a brief memorial service in the car. I figured that was better than saying a prayer over the toilet—the fish's final resting place. I took every precaution to make sure that Hannah was okay, that she would not be emotionally scarred by this potentially traumatic experience. I explained that goldfish are fragile creatures and that even though they don't live long lives, we need to love and care for them as long as they are with us. She turned to me and said, "I just want another fish."

I then e-mailed her parents to tell them everything that had happened. I explained how I had dealt with the situation and assured them that a new fish was in the works. Her father e-mailed back with a comforting, "Really, thanks for working so hard and keeping up with this....MURDERER!"

The next day, feeling about as low as a human being can possibly feel, I went back to the pet store and asked for a fish that would live longer than the previous one—at least a week, so her parents would be home and could claim responsibility for any untimely demise. This time I left with a betta fish, a beautiful blue Siamese fighting fish, which I can only hope is more resilient than its American cousin.

The other day in carpool, I asked Hannah enthusiastically, "How's your fish doing?"

"He's good," she responded. "He's still living."

I smiled, realizing that a pet fish really is a wonderful way to teach lessons about life, love, and loss. I just never imagined that I would be the one learning them.

Trophy Wife

I KNOW THAT COMPETITION IS SUPPOSED TO BE GOOD FOR THE SOUL, BUT I'm not so sure it's good for me and my soul mate.

Both of us are competitive. We both like to win, and, most of all, we both hate to lose. However, Alan happens to be a more gracious winner, and I happen to be a far worse loser. (These are not attributes I'm proud of, let me assure you.)

To add salt to my wounded competitive streak is the fact that Alan is also a super athlete—not just like super great at sports, but like Superman. He has run marathons, raced in triathlons, completed an Iron Man competition, and biked a 145-mile stage of the Tour de France. Plus, he is an excellent water-skier, snowboarder, tennis player, golfer, and swimmer, and he can pick up any sport in a matter of minutes.

I, on the other hand, am really good at Scrabble.

So although I have always considered myself reasonably athletic and coordinated, it was clear early in our relationship that Alan's athleticism was by all measures out of my league. As a result, when it comes to sports, he has always been my mentor, not my tormentor.

Except for the time we played ping-pong.

When Alan and I were first married, his mom gave us the old ping-pong table from his childhood home. The first day we got it, we immediately set it up, and Alan challenged me to a game. My eyes lit up—he was throwing down the proverbial paddle, and I was ready to accept. I saw this as an opportunity to prove my own athletic prowess. I mean, it was ping-pong, right? I had a fighting chance.

The first game was close. Alan beat me by only a few points. The second game was even closer; my adrenaline was pumping, and I was getting into my groove until he aced me and won with a curve ball. Halfway through the third game, I was totally in the zone, concentrating on every point, ready to return anything he sent over the net. And then he threw me the *real* curve ball.

He paused and gave me a sly smile I'll never forget. Bobbing from side to side, sweat pouring down my face, I nodded and smiled back as a way of acknowledging this cordial break in play—all the while thinking how badly I wanted to make him beg for mercy.

He stood there a few more seconds and finally said, "I know something you don't know."

I smiled back. "Oh really? And what is that?"

He tossed the ping-pong paddle from his left hand—the hand he had been using the whole time—to his right hand. "I'm really right-handed," he said.

That's when our healthy competition took a sudden turn for the worse. It was just like that scene in the movie *The Princess Bride*, when Inigo Montoya is sword-fighting with Westley, and they both switch hands and admit they had been fighting with their weaker side. Except in this scenario, *I was already using my stronger side!* I had nothing. I was so annoyed and infuriated and embarrassed that I threw my paddle onto the table, yelled, "Game over!" and walked out of the room. To this day, we have never played ping-pong against each other again.

Over the past ten years I can count on one hand (okay, two fingers) the times I've beaten my husband at anything remotely athletic. Once was playing two-on-two basketball when we were at the beach, about four years ago. The other time was when I beat him at not one, but two games of pool in one night. These are the moments I hold onto when I need confidence and inspiration—like when I came into the kitchen one morning and found three giant trophies lined up on the countertop, massive golden replicas of swimmers and tennis players representing Alan's adolescent athletic prowess. Apparently, it's not enough that he is a stellar adult athlete; he was also some sort of child superstar, as well.

My three boys looked up from their cereal bowls to gaze admiringly at their father's trophies.

"Look at Daddy's trophies, Mommy," Arthur said. "Aren't they awesome?"

Before I could agree, Abe asked, "Where are *your* trophies, Mommy?"

For a moment, I panicked, thinking about the multitude of standard six-inch trophies I had collected throughout elementary school, the type they give every child for participation, that eventually ended up in the Goodwill pile. Then I looked back at my boys' proud faces.

"My trophies are sitting at the table, eating breakfast," I said. Because even though my husband and I make lousy competitors, we make incredible teammates.

Besides, it's not my fault they don't give out trophies for Scrabble.

Raising Cane

THERE IS PROBABLY NOTHING MORE DISCONCERTING FOR A PARENT THAN finding out that your child is being bullied at school—except, perhaps, finding out that your child *is* the bully at school. Especially when the bully in question is your two-year-old.

Levi is the youngest of our three boys, and this past summer, he started preschool. One of my favorite things about his school is the daily report that we get from his teacher. From one concise sheet of paper, I learn everything about Levi's day, from his participation in circle time and musical activities to his mood and the number of times he went potty. It's the preschool equivalent of *Headline News*.

Every so often, there might be a short note at the bottom of the sheet, usually requesting additional supplies for Levi's cubby or reminding parents of an upcoming special program at school. But a few weeks ago, that "note" was a page and a half long. As soon as I saw all the writing on the paper, I could also see the writing on the wall—Levi was in trouble.

The first two sentences were all I needed to read to confirm my suspicions: "Levi is usually a happy and sweet-tempered little guy, and we enjoy having him in class. Today, though, Levi did punch his friend in the face repeatedly."

The first thing I thought was, "Great. My son will now be known around school as 'the puncher.'" Fortunately, Levi's preschool has a strict anonymity policy, presumably designed to keep the assailant's reputation intact by keeping the identities of both victim and attacker anonymous to the parents.

Theoretically this is a fool-proof policy—unless, of course, your four-year-old son happens to attend the same preschool and serves as the town crier. Before I could read further, Abe ran down the school hall, yelling, "Levi punched Jake at school today, Mommy! He punched him in the face, and then he got put in time-out! He really did!"

So much for the preschool protection plan.

Unable to decide who was more deserving of a stern look, the puncher or the crier, I read more of the teacher's note:

"This is the first time we have had any punching in our classroom, so I don't think he picked it up from another child here. When I asked him about what happened, he said that he'd 'punched' his friend … we haven't used the word 'punch' in our class before, so I was surprised he knew it. He seemed very pleased with himself about it."

The second thought that crossed my mind was, "Great. Now I'm going to be known as the parent of the kid who punches." Why couldn't he be a biter?

No one particularly likes a biter, but everyone knows it's not the parent's fault; people feel sympathy for the parent of a biter. No one likes a hitter. And I can't imagine what they would think of a puncher—especially when this particular puncher happens to be the toddler version of Goliath, easily a head or two taller than the rest of his classmates. Plus, his teacher clearly implied in her note that this was behavior learned at home. So not only did my child beat up another kid, but also it was quite obviously my fault.

That night I sat down with Levi on his bed, and just as his teacher suggested, I took his hands in mine and said calmly, "These are nice hands, Levi, and we only use them to do nice things. Did you hit one of your friends today?"

He looked at me with the face of an angel and said, "No, I didn't hit, I *punched* Jake in the face!" Then he smiled. And before I could repeat the "nice hands" mantra a second time, Levi was off his bed and wrestling with his brothers.

While Alan and I don't condone violence in our house, we do allow occasional rough-housing among the boys. And while we have a zero-tolerance policy for bad words or disrespectful language, we might encourage a playful pillow fight or a tackling contest. Levi lives in a punch-or-be-punched world, surrounded by brothers who often show their affection through action. This, I realized, was possibly Levi's way of showing that same affection for his friend Jake.

The next morning, I sent a note back to Levi's teacher assuring her that my husband and I would work with her to see that this behavior didn't occur again. I then took Levi's hands in mine, and this time I said to him the one thing I knew he would understand:

"These are nice hands, Levi, and we only use them to do nice things. And if you promise not to punch any of your friends in school today, I'll let you tackle your brothers when you get home." He smiled and said, "Okay, Mommy."

The good news is that Levi hasn't punched anyone in his class since. The bad news is that last night he tried to tackle his grandmother.

Micromothering

WHEN I BECAME A MOTHER, I ALSO BECAME A MICROMANAGER. I'M not proud of it; that's just the way it is. As a parent, I am constantly torn between wanting my children to be independent and wanting them to do things the right way—okay, *my* way. So I find myself constantly trying to tweak, fix, adjust, nudge, correct, and suggest different ways for them to act, talk, behave, or just be. It is tireless and thankless work, I can assure you.

On any given day, at any given moment, I find myself fine-tuning the strings of my sons' lives. *Sit up straight. Use your fork. Wipe your mouth. Eat your broccoli. Don't eat that! Did you wash your hands? With soap? Say please. Say thank you. Say you're welcome. Look them in the eye. Speak up. Lower your voice. Hug your uncle. Kiss your grandmother. Slow down. Walk faster. Don't run. Don't pick on your brother. Don't pick your nose. Just … Don't … Say … Do … That … No …* Arggggggggh! It is never-ending.

But just when I thought it couldn't get any worse, I hit rock bottom. I went from being a micromanager to a micro*monster*. And it wasn't pretty.

A few months ago, our six-year-old, Arthur, got his first Webkinz. In case you've been lucky enough to avoid this furry fad, Webkinz are the newest craze to hit the kids' consumer market, plush pets that come to life on the Web. Each toy comes with a secret code that lets you adopt your pet in Webkinz World. You choose its name and gender, and then you're off to instant parenthood. You get a virtual room for your pet and two thousand dollars in virtual money—KinzCash—which you use to buy virtual furniture, virtual food, and other virtual items to keep your pet healthy and happy.

Two weeks after getting his Webkinz, Arthur was virtually broke. He had spent all but twenty-one dollars of his KinzCash on a million things for his pet's room, and he was complaining that he didn't have enough money in his bank to buy an additional room for his pet lion. It was more than I could bear.

So one night, while the boys were asleep, I decided to take a casual stroll around Webkinz World. As I innocently perused the different venues, Arthur's twenty-one dollars in KinzCash was glaring at me from the corner. Begging me for help. I decided just to check out Quizzy's Question Corner, where you can answer a series of questions and win instant KinzCash. I figured I would answer a few questions, maybe add a few dollars to Arthur's bank. Besides, I wasn't doing it just for Arthur; I was doing it for the poor lion. I couldn't let my Grandkinz live in a one-room shanty, could I? I would just answer a few simple questions and be in and out in a few minutes, tops. An hour later, I looked down and saw that Arthur now had well over five hundred dollars, more than enough to buy a second room—and to blow my cover. But what was done was done.

Arthur didn't go on his site for nearly a week. When he finally asked if he could play Webkinz for a few minutes, I started to confess what I had done, but instead just nodded him toward the computer, thinking maybe he wouldn't even notice.

That night at dinner, Arthur said, "Mommy, you won't believe this. When you don't go on Webkinz World for a few days, you actually *make* money. I had twenty-one dollars in there, and now I have, like, five hundred!"

The guilt was too much to bear; I had to come clean. I admitted to Arthur all that I had done—that I wanted him to have enough money for a room, that I sneaked onto the site and played games and won the money myself. I told him I was only doing it for him and that it was wrong and that I was really, really sorry.

He stared at me across the table, not saying a word. I finally asked, "Are you mad?"

He thought about it a second and replied, "Nah. I'm not mad, Mommy." And then he added, "But, do you think you can go back on my site tonight? How about every night?"

It was at that moment that I realized if I ever wanted my boys to become men, my micromanaging days needed to come to an end. I needed to let my sons make their own mistakes so they would appreciate their own successes. I would still be there to offer advice, of course, but I wanted them to do things their way, not my way, from now on. "No, Honey," I said. "I can't go on there again. From now on, you do whatever you want, because it's your site. And I'm really sorry for being so bossy, too."

Arthur looked at me and said, "You're not bossy, Mommy. You're the perfect woman." And for once, all I could manage was a smile.

Ho, Ho, Chanukah

S O HERE IT IS, THE TOKEN CHANUKAH ARTICLE. YOU KNEW IT WAS COMING. With all those swans a-swimming and geese a-laying and maids a-milking this time of year, you just knew that dreidel would come a-spinning sooner or later.

You remember Chanukah, right? It's that Jewish holiday that conveniently falls right in the middle of December, that once was considered only mildly important by members of the tribe, but that seems to gain in fame and recognition every year—thanks to its very merry counterpart.

The difference, of course, is that Christmas is truly a sacred religious holiday. In fact, Christmas and Easter on the Christian calendar are the equivalent of Rosh Hashanah and Yom Kippur on the Jewish one. On the other hand, Chanukah is kind of like Flag Day on the secular calendar—it's fun to celebrate, but hey, it's no Fourth of July.

And so every year around this time, my husband and I are faced with two important challenges. First, how do we ensure that our children feel confident in their beliefs during this holiday season? And second, how do we ensure that our children understand that Chanukah is a celebration of a time when our people fought for religious freedom, and not a festival we made up so we could compete for the "coolest holiday" prize?

This is the gist of any given conversation with any one of our three sons during the weeks leading up to Christmas:

Me: So, what do you say if someone asks you what you want for Christmas this year?

Son: I would tell them I want Pokémon cards and roller blades.

Me: No, Honey, remember? We don't celebrate Christmas, we celebrate Chanukah.

Son: Oh, yeah. But what if Santa gets confused and goes down our chimney by mistake?

Me: I can promise you that won't happen. Santa is very smart. He knows we're Jewish.

Son: Well, that's okay, because we get presents for eight days and some people only get presents for one day, so we're really lucky, right, Mom?

Me: Well, that's true, but I don't think you should say that. It's not nice to brag.

Son: Okay. Sorry.

This all seems like a solid plan until it is actually put into action. Last year around this time, I took our two older boys, Arthur and Abe, who were six and four, to get their hair cut, and I brought along their best friend, Hannah. As the hairdresser was cutting Arthur's hair, she casually asked, "So, are you excited about Christmas?" to which Arthur happily replied, "Yes, I am." At that moment, Hannah quickly intervened, saying, "Actually, he doesn't celebrate Christmas, he celebrates Chanukah. He's Jewish." I watched as Arthur's cheeks turned bright red and he sank lower into his chair. The hairstylist stared for a second and then resumed cutting, making no further small talk.

On the way home, I couldn't stop thinking about what had just transpired. Was my son ashamed of being Jewish? Afraid to be different? Why didn't he say what Hannah had said for him? I finally asked, "Arthur, when that woman asked if you were excited about Christmas, why did you say yes?" He looked at me with a sweet innocence and said, "Mom, I know I don't celebrate Christmas, but I *am* excited about it." It was that simple.

And it reminded me that being Jewish in a non-Jewish world is sometimes challenging and complex, sort of like being sober at a Grateful Dead concert. You might feel different or out of place at times, but if you spend the whole time concentrating on what everyone else is doing, if you only focus on the crowd, you just end up missing out on the music. (Wow, that was deep.)

The point is, if my children get excited about Christmas, I don't blame them. The lights, the music, the mall Santas—it's all very exciting, I agree. I just want them to be proud of who they are and what they believe while respecting other people's beliefs and traditions. I want them to know that holidays are not about getting presents, they are about giving to others. And they're not about counting all the things we want, they're about counting all the blessings we have.

And most of all, I want them to know that in July 1995, I saw Jerry Garcia's last show with the Grateful Dead in Chicago. It was one of the best concerts I have ever seen—and I was sober the whole time. Happy holidays.

Crash Course

W HENEVER ALAN LEAVES TO GO ON A BUSINESS TRIP, HE KISSES OUR three boys good-bye and says to our oldest, "While Daddy is gone, you are the man of the house. Look after Mommy and your brothers, okay?" And in between bites of cereal and thumbing his Nintendo, Arthur manages to give at least a nod, as if to say, "Yeah, Dad, I'm on it."

Even though our children are relatively young—three, five, and seven—I do take comfort in knowing that they are around when my husband is not, and that they ultimately will take care of their mommy. I figure at the very least, this instinct is innate, especially in boys. I have always imagined that the words "Protect my mama" are somehow encoded onto their DNA.

This theory was further validated when I recently heard a story on the radio about a two-year-old boy who saved his mother's life. Apparently his mother had passed out, and the toddler responded quickly by dialing 911 and simply telling the operator, "Mommy down!" After hearing that amazing tale, I realized that while the instinct to save me might come naturally to my children, the ability to call for help is, in fact, a learned trait. I had some serious work to do.

So the next day, I put my sons through "911 Boot Camp." We role-played the various situations that would require them to call this emergency number, and I assured them that none of these involved running low on Lucky Charms or cable going out. Once they understood what constitutes an emergency, they practiced dialing the number (on a disconnected phone), talking to the operator (me), and relating all relevant information. By the end of our little practice session, all three boys felt confident in their ability to act in an emergency, and I felt confident that I had successfully trained my own personal rescue squad.

But just as any true emergency is impossible to predict, I never could have imagined what would occur just a few weeks later. It was 7:15 a.m. on a Wednesday. Alan was out of town on another business trip, and I was engaged in the typical morning routine: fixing breakfast, packing lunches, and loading backpacks. In the midst of this organized chaos, I realized we were out of waffles. "Be right back," I called to the boys, as I headed to the basement to retrieve more from the extra freezer.

At the top of the stairs, I miscalculated the first step and literally rolled down the entire flight, letting out a sharp scream on the way down. After coming to a crashing halt, I lay still for a moment, taking inventory to make sure nothing was broken. Luckily, I was fine—which was a relief, because I knew that any minute, all three boys would come running down the stairs, scared and worried that their mother was hurt.

Yes, any minute now, they would come running down the stairs. To check on me. Their poor, helpless mother. Any minute, now …

But no one came. Not a single voice even called out to ask, "Are you okay, Mom?" That's when a new kind of panic set in—the kind that slapped me in the face and made me realize that unless one of those boys ran out of milk or needed his bottom wiped, they might have left me lying on the basement floor forever.

After a few lonely and somewhat painful moments, I picked myself up and set forth on my original mission for frozen waffles. I returned to the kitchen to find a scene exactly as I had left it—three little boys busy coloring, eating, and playing Nintendo, as if nothing unusual had transpired.

"Excuse me," I said as I walked back into the room, "but did anyone hear me fall down the stairs and scream a few minutes ago?"

They all looked up, a little perplexed by my question, until one finally asked, "That was you? Are you okay, Mommy?"

Just as I was about to lecture them about how they shamelessly ignored their poor mother, and how I might have been really hurt and could have broken my leg, I stopped myself. Instead, I simply responded, "Yeah, I'm fine." Their duty is not to rescue me, I thought; my duty is to make sure I am always there to rescue them. I am the emergency service they call when they need help. And luckily, some days all that means is finding a few more frozen waffles.

Don't I Know You?

THERE IS SOMETHING I HAVE BEEN DESPERATELY WANTING TO GET OFF MY chest, so I thought I would just come right out and say it: I have no idea who you are.

Yes, you. Reading this column. Who are you? Where did we meet? How do I know you? And what the heck is your name? Please don't take this personally. It's not you; it's me. I just can't remember you.

I used to think I was just really bad at names, but lately I have come to the conclusion that I am really bad at remembering things in general, and names in particular. My rationale is that the brain can hold only so much information, and currently mine is filled with episodes of *American Idol* and *Lost*. So unless your name is Simon or Sawyer, I have no more memory left for you or your face.

Over the years, I've learned a few tricks to mask that uncomfortable, panicked moment when I see someone familiar approaching and am drawing a blank on his or her identity. My favorite is what I have dubbed "the Seinfeld approach." You may remember the episode: Jerry forgets this woman's name, so he gives her a friendly grin and says, "Well, hey *you*." It's a perfect cover, and one I find myself using several times over the course of a week.

My backup plan is helpful 93 percent of the time, but it requires the presence of a third party whose name I do know. Let's say the person who is standing with me and whose name I have committed to memory is Jane. Jane … something. I can't remember her last name. Anyway, when person X approaches, I smile, greet him or her in a generic fashion, and then casually ask, "Oh, do you know Jane?" At that point, person X will usually introduce him or herself to Jane, and that potential moment of embarrassment is successfully averted.

Of course, there is that 7 percent chance that person X already knows Jane, or that person X might simply reply, "Hi, nice to see you"—without ever offering a name. However, 52 percent of the time, Jane is savvy enough to catch on to my plan and the impending doom and will interject, "I'm sorry, I didn't catch your name." Way to go, Jane! So if you factor the 93 percent by the 52 percent and multiply by the 7 percent, then realistically you have something like a 391 percent chance of getting by in life without ever knowing a single person's name.

My father had a backup for this backup plan, which I cannot honestly recommend, but which I will share with you in case of a dire emergency. He once ran into a guy whose name he could not recall. There was no third party present to help salvage the wreckage that would ultimately ensue. A good fifteen minutes into the conversation, person X called Dad's bluff and asked, "Do you have any idea what my name is?" To which Dad quickly replied, "Sure I do, but if you've forgotten, that's pretty bad!"

Lately, I haven't been forgetting people's names, because apparently I haven't even bothered to learn them in the first place. The other day, a woman came up to me after a meeting, introduced herself, and then enthusiastically added that she was Ian Brown's aunt. My blank stare must have given away the fact that I had no idea whom she was talking about, so she repeated herself. "Ian Brown? He's three years old? He goes to preschool with your son?"

"Ohhhhhhh," I said, trying to maintain some semblance of recognition. "Of course, Ian. Sorry, I blanked for a moment."

The truth was, I didn't blank. I had no idea who Ian Brown was. But what I did know was that for the past two years, my youngest son has had two best friends in his preschool, Jake and Ian. And until that very moment, I had no idea that either of them had a last name. (By the way, Ian's last name is not really Brown. I could say I used a pseudonym to protect his identity, but the truth is, I just can't remember it.)

I do feel bad about the blank stares, the desperate pneumonic devices, and the fact that I sometimes call my children Hershey, who is our dog. But I hope you know that the next time I see you on the street or in a restaurant or in a store or even at that place where we met that one time, I really am genuinely happy to see you. Whoever you are.

The Oys of Summer

WITH THE FIRST DAY OF SCHOOL FAST APPROACHING AND ANOTHER summer coming to a close, I think I speak on behalf of parents everywhere when I say, "Hallelujah! It's about time!"

This has been, by far, the hardest, longest, most tiring, and most trying three months of my life. Do you know what I have had to do for the past seventy-nine days? I have had to entertain my children. Constantly. And that takes a lot of work. Let's just say that three boys, seven camps, and one swim team later, I am ready for summer to be o-ver.

I never thought I would hear those words come out of my mouth. I *loved* summer as a kid. It meant longer days and later nights. Sleeping in. Going out. Swimming until my skin was pruned. Camp. Friends. Fun. And watching TV—lots and lots of TV. Summer used to be the best part of my year. Now it is the bane of my existence.

My routine has been put through the ringer. The children who used to be asleep by eight are up until midnight. Three meals a day has somehow evolved into thirty. And I have turned into a twenty-four-hour taxi service, shuttling little people around every minute of every day, from home to camp to home again, only to hear, "We're bored." So we pack up, go swimming, and then eat and swim and then eat some more and, well, thank goodness for the chlorinated pool, because at least my kids don't have to take a bath every night. Or ever. Who has time for a bath, anyway, when you get home at 8:30 p.m. and Mom says, "Sure, you can watch a movie tonight. It's summer!" and it ends up being the 1977 version of *Star Wars*—which is about an hour longer than she remembered?

And as if the usual trials and tribulations of a summer schedule weren't tedious enough, my husband signed up our oldest son for swim team again.

Oh joy. Oh bliss. Oh happy day.

For those of you who have been lucky enough to avoid swim team thus far in your parenting careers, let me give you the CliffsNotes version of this sport:

Imagine your kid has been awake and active for twelve hours straight and is completely exhausted, cranky, and ready for bed (as are you)—and now you must tell him to put on his bathing suit because he's going to swim laps for sixty to ninety minutes. He shows you the cut on his foot and says he can't possibly swim. You get him a waterproof Band-Aid. He says he doesn't feel like swimming. You say that's too bad. He cries. You walk him to the edge of the pool and give a knowing nod to the coach, as if to say, "He's all yours." Then *you* cry because you just realized the pool concession stand closed at 7:00 p.m. and you have nothing to drink. This is called "swim team practice."

Now take that same cranky, whiny, tired child, a few towels, and a cooler of random snacks from your pantry, and drag them all to a different pool, where there is nowhere to sit except on the hot cement in the sun surrounded by dozens of other cranky, whiny, tired children forced to be there by their equally cranky, whiny, tired parents. Tell your child he gets to swim three times, for a total of ninety seconds—but he will have to stay at the pool for four hours straight, and you can offer no rational explanation why. This is called a "swim meet."

My husband and I were both avid swimmers when we were young. But while he and his siblings were on serious swim teams, I was just serious about swimming. The only team my friends and I cared about was the one we created those summers at the neighborhood pool. We needed endurance to play a game of sharks and minnows, not to swim a lap of freestyle. We raced across the pool to get away from the boys, not in lanes against each other. Instead of diving at meets, we were diving for pennies. The only timers we had were the lifeguards, who called for a ten-minute break each hour, and our parents, who told us when it was time to leave. And the only judges we cared about were our friends, who decided who held the longest underwater handstand or who had the best dive off the three-meter board.

Don't get me wrong: overall this was a great summer, and swim team was a positive experience. I just want my children to remember their summers as fondly as I remember my own. I want them to long for summer days, not dread the summer schedule. I want them to have the same laid-back, let-'em-do-what-they-want kind of summer that every child needs and deserves. And I want that darned concession stand to stay open until at least 7:30 p.m.

The Circle of Lice

THERE ARE A LOT OF THINGS YOU'D NEVER WANT TO HEAR SOMEONE utter about your child. Among them would be the phrase, *Your son has lice.*

I know—just reading the word makes me itch, too. There is nothing more disgusting than the thought of lice, except for the reality of lice on your children and in your house. So when two of our sons were sent home from school with that diagnosis, you can imagine my joy.

The last and only time I had ever dealt with lice was when I was eleven years old and at overnight camp. As far as I knew, lice were something you could catch only while sharing a cabin in the middle of the woods with a dozen prepubescent girls. Apparently, however, elementary schools in the suburbs are not immune.

The challenge with lice—sorry, I need to scratch again—is how to treat them, because unfortunately there is no obvious or universal remedy. If the boys have a fever, I give them Tylenol and a cool rag. If they have an upset stomach, I give them ginger ale and a trash can. But when they come home with microscopic bugs in their hair, I can only offer them a blank stare and a shudder.

So the first thing I did, right after putting the boys in their room and sealing their door frame with Saran Wrap, was to hit the drugstore. Just because *I* didn't know how to treat lice didn't mean a treatment didn't exist. And there, on the bottom shelf of the shampoo aisle, I found just what I was looking for: the #1 head lice treatment solution used by professionals. I know this, because it said so right on the box. Then I noticed that it said that on *every* box. So I bought them all. I figured if one treatment was great, then five would be even better.

I followed the directions to a tee. I shampooed and rinsed and combed and gelled and combed again, and then I just prayed that the suckers were gone. But not before stripping the boys' beds, washing their clothes, vacuuming their rooms, bagging their stuffed animals, and tearing my own hair out. After five hours of disinfecting my kids and my house, I knew why lice were one of the ten plagues. I also knew it would not be easy to set my little people free.

After treating the boys, I decided it would be smart to check myself, just in case. Even if all my itching and scratching was psychosomatic, it was making me psycho. So I attempted to do a lice check on my own head, but the only white things I could find were either dandruff or gray hairs. Somehow, that was comforting.

A week after trying every known over-the-counter cure-in-a-box I could find, the lice were back. Or maybe they never left. Either way, I was at a total loss. Aside from shaving my kids' heads and burning down my house, I really didn't know what to do. So I did what any mature woman and mother of three would do in this situation: I called my mommy.

She told me to call my uncle in New York. Apparently his daughter has had lice not once, but three times. "And they live on the Upper East Side," Mom added—as if that were supposed to make me feel better. So I left my uncle a desperate voicemail: "Call me. I hear you are the expert on lice, and I need your help!"

Lice are so difficult to eliminate because they are nearly impossible to see. In fact, there is no way I would have known that my children even had lice if the school secretary hadn't shown me that tiny speck on a hair shaft that I would have assumed was, well, just a tiny speck. I cannot stand bugs of any variety, but I'd much rather have a cockroach problem than a lice infestation. At least I would be able to tell if there were cockroaches in my hair.

Since the medicated formulas didn't work, I bought an array of what I had determined to be the top home and organic remedies. I now have a wealth of them under my bathroom sink, including tea tree oil shampoo, Denorex, baby oil, Neem oil, and Listerine. I also bought a magnifying glass (and by the way, under a magnifying glass, *everything* looks like a bug) and this special comb called the LiceMeister, because it is, of course, the only comb endorsed by the National Pediculosis Association. Don't even ask me what that is.

Just when I thought I had reached my lice limit, my uncle returned my call. I was certain he would have the perfect words of wisdom, until he said, "So, you think I'm an expert on life, huh?"

"LICE!" I yelled into the phone. "I said you are the expert on LICE, not life."

He suggested a steel comb and a lot of patience.

At this point, I'd settle for a shampoo that controls dandruff and covers my grays. As for the lice, I'm sure I will be able to take that Saran Wrap off the boys' door any day now.

The Boy Who Cried Full

I AM SURE YOU KNOW THE STORY OF THE BOY WHO CRIED WOLF. SO LET ME tell you a lesser-known tale about The Boy Who Cried Full.

Fortunately, I'm not the mother of picky eaters. I am the mother of just one picky eater—our four-year-old son, Levi. His three favorite foods are hot dogs, pizza, and ketchup. And yes, apparently ketchup is a food.

Nevertheless, in our house there is a long-standing dinnertime decree that you will eat whatever is being served. If you want something else, you must fix it yourself. As a matter of principle, I refuse to accommodate five individual tastes by cooking five separate meals. (Frankly, they're lucky if I even get around to cooking one.)

And it's not like I'm a gourmet, either. I usually offer up a meat, starch, and vegetable option at any given meal. Sometimes it's as simple as tuna fish or grilled chicken. And when my husband goes out of town, I subscribe to the "breakfast for dinner" plan: Lucky Charms for everyone! You get the idea.

Even though my family fully understands that in our house "what you see is what you get," at least once a week, as I put a plate of food in front of Levi, he'll screech, "What? I didn't order that!" To which I usually respond, "This is the Lebovitz house, not the Waffle House, dude. Eat it."

The scene that ensues is always the same:

Levi will pick at his peas, stab at his steak, and mess around with his mashed potatoes, so it looks like he's actually eaten something. After a few minutes of pointless prodding, he will declare, "I'm done. Can I have dessert now?" I will look at his plate and say, "You are not done, and only boys who make a happy plate will get dessert." (I know—even *I* can't believe I really use that line.) Then I prepare myself for his dramatic finish, as he insists, "But I'm FUUUUUUULLL!" As if making him eat another bite on a full stomach is just plain torture.

But since I am a mother and therefore smarter and always one step ahead, I retort, "Great. If you're full, then you don't need to eat dessert." And that's when I hear the ten-minute lecture on Levi's level of fullness—how he isn't all-the-way full, just enough full to be able to eat dessert, but how if I make him all-the-way full, then he really won't have room for dessert, and wouldn't that be a shame.

In the event that Levi's very passionate plea is not persuasive enough, he has one last trick in his belly: "But I have a stomachache!" At which point I usually send him crying to his room, where he no doubt sneaks a Kit Kat or some other treat he has been hiding under his bed since Halloween.

So it came as no surprise when, a few weeks ago, we went out to dinner with the grandparents and, in the middle of eating his pasta with sauce, Levi decided he was done. The battle and the bargaining began, ending predictably with his insistent, "I'm FUUUUUUULLL, and I have a stomachache." A small tantrum and a few tears later, I broke down and agreed to take him home early.

"But you don't get dessert, and you're going straight to bed," I threatened, to make sure he was committed to the plan.

"Will you at least read me a book?" he asked.

"Faker!" I thought to myself.

And then, about a mile from our house, Levi started complaining that his throat hurt. And then he said that he felt like he was choking.

"Choking?" I asked. "Do you think you're going to …"

But just as the words were leaving my mouth, Levi's dinner was leaving his. He threw up all over my car, and by the time we got home just a few minutes later, he had thrown up twice more. I felt sick to my stomach—and not just because there was pasta and sauce all over my floorboards. My baby was legitimately sick, and the whole time I'd thought he was just crying, "Full!"

I apologized to Levi profusely and throughout the night, as he was up every hour for the next ten hours. And, to his credit, only once did he say, "I told you I had a stomachache, Mommy."

The next morning, still writhing in guilt, I let him lie on the couch and watch cartoons all day. I even set up a TV tray and gave him Sprite to drink. But I knew we were both on the road to recovery when I gently put a blanket over him, placed a warm toasted bagel with butter in front of him, and said, "There you go, Levi. I love you." To which he responded, "What? I didn't order that!"

Party Pooper

A LL PROFESSIONALS HAVE THAT ONE SEASON OF THE YEAR THEY TEND to dread—a time when things seem especially busy and life is just a bit more complicated. For accountants, it's tax season. For retailers, it's the holiday season. For moms, it's the birthday season. Right now, I am in the midst of mine.

Our three boys were born in March, May, and June, so in that brief span we host three separate, unique, and high-maintenance birthday parties. And every year they seem to get more complicated and less fun—at least for me. These days, organizing a kid's birthday party is like hosting a major event. Give me a thousand-person fundraiser to plan over a six-year-old's birthday party any day. At least those results are measurable.

When I was young, the formula for any decent birthday party was pretty basic: Activity + Silly Hats + Birthday Cake + Ice Cream = Fun. Today, that formula looks more like a calculus equation than an addition problem.

For one thing, it seems like every party has to have a theme. I always thought the very nature of any party *was* the theme. The theme of a swimming party is swimming. The theme of a roller-skating party is roller skating. The theme of a bowling party is bowling. Get the picture? Instead, I find myself throwing parties that shamelessly promote some movie, Disney character, or TV show. I just hope I don't owe royalties on any of the invitations I have created along the way, like when I substituted the heads of all four of The Wiggles and Captain Feathersword with the heads of our five family members. (If you are wondering who The Wiggles are, consider yourself lucky.)

And what is the deal with piñatas? Seriously, who decided this would be an appropriate game for children? My idea of a good time is not blindfolding a dozen five-year-olds, handing each of them a large stick, and then letting them loose.

My all-time favorite piñata story was when someone I know bought a piñata for her son's sixth birthday party and didn't realize she had to fill it with candy herself. After the kids had successfully pummeled that poor piñata to death and it finally split in two, they frantically ran with their bags in tow to collect the goods, only to stop in their tracks and stare in disbelief at the bare floor. They looked into the empty belly of the colorful beast, and then at the mom, hoping for some viable explanation. She could only shrug her shoulders and say, "Sorry, kids. My bad." Her son will never let her live that one down.

Unfortunately for her, the piñata was not only a primary party activity; it was also the source for her goody bags. Which brings up my next question: Who invented the goody bag, and has that person been hunted down and shot? I thought the point of celebrating someone's birthday was to give, not to receive. If there's anything worse than getting a bag full of junk at the end of a soiree, it's leaving with a gift that's better than the one you brought.

I will admit to being a goody bag hypocrite. I am one of those moms who support a universal ban on goody bags, yet I still find myself handing them out each year. Ironically, lots of kids these days, including my own, ask for donations instead of birthday presents from their friends. I feel so good when I bring something that will be donated to a local animal shelter or school, and then feel ridiculous when we go home with a bag of cheap plastic toys that I would just as soon donate to Goodwill. My husband, the most vocal anti-goody-bag crusader I know, has insisted that we put an end to this pathetic practice. He will even call our friends before one of *their* kid's birthday parties to negotiate a goody-bag-free environment.

With one birthday party down and two to go this season, I realize that the end of one celebration is really just the beginning of planning for the next. Luckily, I already found a Darth Vader piñata for the Star Wars-themed bowling and sleepover party we'll be hosting in a few weeks. I just hope I remember to fill it this time.

A Tattle Tale

M Y HUSBAND AND I HAVE ALWAYS TOLD OUR THREE BOYS THAT THEY CAN tell us anything. But lately we have started to second-guess that decision, because instead of confiding in us about certain things, they are bombarding us with everything. In the process, we have created three tenacious tattletales.

Dealing with a tattletale is a somewhat precarious proposition. Discriminating between when one should share something with others and when one should keep something to oneself is often difficult, even for adults. And even though this is theoretically a learned ability that develops as we mature, some people never grow out of the need to "tattle" on others. Indeed, the young tattletale often grows up to be the adult gossip.

When our boys were younger, Alan and I actually encouraged tattling. As Bill Cosby used to say in his stand-up routine, we had our own little "informers" who would accurately fill us in on all the misdeeds of their brothers. And, conveniently, they would often tattle on themselves.

Why is your little brother crying?
Because he fell.
How did he fall?
Because I pushed him.

But over time, occasional tattling has grown into relentless reporting. "He's sitting in my seat." "He called me a baby." "He said he brushed his teeth, but he really didn't." "Well, he peed in his pants and hid his underwear so you wouldn't find out."

"Enough!" I finally yelled one night. "Let me tell you something—I am DONE with all the tattling!"

At that point, Alan walked into the room and asked, "What's going on?"

"Mommy just yelled at us," Abe tattled.

It's rare moments like these when desperation turns into inspiration.

"Who wants an ice cream sundae?" I asked. Every hand in the room immediately shot up. Including Alan's.

"Okay," I said, "I'll make you a deal. If you can go a whole week without tattling on each other, then you will be able to earn an ice cream sundae."

I then borrowed a little incentive that my son's third-grade teacher had used to teach his students their times tables. I told the boys that for every day they went without tattling, they would earn one ingredient towards an ice cream sundae. Day one would earn them a bowl. Day two they would get a scoop of ice cream. Day three, hot fudge. Day four, sprinkles. Day five, M&Ms. Day six, whipped cream. And day seven was, of course, the cherry on top. They had to earn each thing, each day, to get the whole sundae, I explained.

"What about the spoon? How do we earn the spoon?" our five-year-old, Levi, was quick to ask. I eyed him and said, "I'll give you the spoon for free. That way, even if you can't make it a single day without tattling, you can at least hope one of your brothers will share his ice cream with you."

Then we talked about the difference between tattling and telling us something of vital importance. If someone was hurt, I explained, we needed to know. If someone was picking his nose, we didn't really care.

I predicted that Levi would be the first to crack. And, in fact, the very next morning he stood outside my shower, whining that he needed to tell me something. I poked my head out and asked, "Are you *sure* you need to tell me something, and that you won't be tattling?" He immediately winced and seemed to writhe in pain, more tortured by the thought of not tattling than by whatever one of his brothers had apparently done to him. "Do you *really* want to leave this competition with just a spoon?" I added. He turned, bowed his head, and walked away in defeat.

The boys soon learned that simply informing us about something that might require further explanation was not the same as tattling but often yielded the same results—"If you *ask* us what happened, and we tell you, that's not tattling, right Mommy?" I had to give them kudos for their logic.

I knew my plan was really working by midweek, when they woke up in a frenzy, asking, "What day is today? What day is today?" When I responded, "It's Wednesday," they pleaded, "No, is today the hot fudge or the sprinkles?" I smiled and said, "Hot fudge, boys, hot fudge."

The week went by with relative ease and without incident. Or if there were any incidents, we didn't hear about them. By the following Sunday evening, it had been a whole seven days of tattle-free heaven in our home, and Alan and I had relished every moment as much as our children were about to relish their well-earned prize. As our three boys stood side by side at the kitchen counter, politely passing one another the ice cream scoop and generously sharing toppings, I knew this would be one tale I just had to tell.

Clothes Encounters

T HE SCENE IN MY HOUSE THIS MONTH LOOKS ALL TOO FAMILIAR. EMPTY backpacks sit idly by the front door, waiting to be filled. Tennis shoes that have seen better days lie by the staircase, looking tired and tattered. And the clothes that fit our three boys just a few short months ago have been washed and worn beyond recognition and are clearly more suitable for the Build-A-Bears that sit in the corner of the playroom.

I call it "déjà-school." While my children are eagerly preparing to go back to school, I am desperately preparing myself for the dreaded back-to-school shopping.

They always make shopping for back-to-school clothes seem so fun and exciting—"they" being those stores with the splashy window signs, balloon-festooned displays, and employees sporting "Ask me how you can save 20% today" buttons on their lapels. But I am older and wiser for the wear (pun intended); I know it's all a scam. At my house, back-to-school shopping is nothing more than an exercise in torture, as I practice the same retail rituals that generations of mothers before me have endured.

With three boys spaced exactly two years apart, I used to spend every change of season patting myself on the back for having kids who not only are the same gender, but also were born around the same time of year. High five for the hand-me-downs! However, I have found that these well-planned pregnancies no longer mitigate the shopping stress I suffer at the beginning of every school year.

Now, I'm not knocking the pencil-picking, folder-finding, satchel-searching back-to-school shopping that people like my friend Jill look forward to every year. Hey, I love me a Trapper Keeper as much as the next guy. But compared to clothes, shopping for back-to-school supplies is a piece of cake. First, you start out with a very detailed shopping list. Second, you can buy school supplies with relative ease, even with three kids in tow, as long as you come prepared with enough bribes.

But there are not enough M&Ms or Pokémon cards in the world to convince my boys to behave for more than ten minutes at a clothing store. The last time I tried such a bold move, at the Gap, I ended up putting each boy into his own dressing room and literally throwing random pairs of jeans and khakis over their doors, like a zookeeper throwing meat into the lion's den. Since we were taking up the only three dressing rooms in the store, a line started to form, and I eventually had to forgo the separate compartments and cram all three boys into one. We quickly went from the lion's den to the monkey cage and left the store with each boy wearing whatever mismatched outfit happened to fit him, and with me carrying their old clothes in a bag.

I find it particularly frustrating to shop for pants. I'm not sure why they can't properly proportion boys' pants so that a pair that fits their waist will also fit their legs, but apparently that is impossible. My sons will try on pants and, in a nanosecond, will declare, "These are fine," or "Nope, I don't like them." And then I always have to say, "Keep your britches on—I'm not done with you yet," which gives me great pleasure, because I just love any opportunity to use the word *britches* in a sentence. I then carefully eye the pants, make the boys turn around a few times, and tug at their waist, and then, to complete the process, I do the instinctive "crotch pull," at which point they always gasp and demand, "Mom! Why do you have to DO that?" And I always respond, "I have no idea! I think it's just something mothers are supposed to do!"

The other day, it finally hit me: my mother *never* took my siblings and me shopping. She works for a department store, and yet she never once took us there to buy new clothes. Instead, every season she would come home with bags and bags of new clothes and shoes to try on, and she would just return anything that didn't fit. Rather than cramming us into dressing rooms, she would throw all the bags and us into our individual bedrooms. We complained all the same, but at least when we acted up, she didn't have to threaten to send us to our rooms—we were already there. Brilliant.

So now all I have to do is figure out who's grown out of what, who needs what size, and where I can get it all on sale. To make matters more complicated, I am shopping for one boy who is growing at the speed of light, one boy who has a bizarre aversion to seams and tags, and one boy who would just as soon wear no clothes at all.

I wonder if Trapper Keeper is making clothes these days. At least they would be one-size-fits-all.

"The Talk"

A FEW WEEKS AGO, OUR NINE-YEAR-OLD SON APPROACHED ME WITH A very serious and stern look on his face. He paused for a moment and then finally asked, "Mom, can we talk?" My immediate thought was, "Oy! This is it! The talk I have been both anticipating and dreading." I knew this day would come, but I just couldn't believe it was really here. Was Arthur ready for this discussion? And more important, was I?

I did what any good mother in this situation would do. I put on my best "Oprah face," looked my son straight in the eye, and responded, "Of course. What do you want to talk about?"—preparing myself for just about any question he might ask. Except, of course, for the one he did.

"Mom," he said, and then took a deep breath, "I have been really curious about something. When exactly do you think I might … get a cell phone?"

"What?" I asked, somewhat shocked that *this* would be the topic of our very precious mother-and-son discussion.

"A cell phone," he said with added emphasis. "I really want a cell phone, and I was wondering when I might get one."

Even though this wasn't exactly the discussion I anticipated, I took advantage of this opportunity to make it the conversation I wanted to have. I explained to Arthur that he wasn't getting a cell phone now or any time soon. And that maybe he could look forward to getting one when he was sixteen and driving a car, because by then we would definitely want and need to know where he was at all times.

Now it was his turn for shock and disbelief. He looked up and exclaimed, "Sixteen? Are you kidding me? That's forEVER. And by then ALL of my friends will have cell phones except for ME." At which point I shot back with one of those infuriating responses that only a mother would offer, "Well, if *all* your friends have cell phones, then you really won't need one. You can just borrow one of theirs if you need to make a call." And with that he walked off in a huff.

Unfortunately, he stomped away before I could get into my "when I was your age" talk. He missed hearing me reminisce about 1979, when I was nine years old and my biggest concern wasn't whether or not I would get a cell phone, it was whether or not my best friends would let me be Kelly when we played Charlie's Angels. (Or at least anyone but Sabrina!)

We didn't own cell phones or have even a single cordless phone in our house, because they didn't exist. "Privacy" was a term used loosely in our home when it came to phone calls, since our few telephones were all located in public spaces. I always seemed to find myself tethered to the kitchen wall during the most private conversations of my formative years, and walking back and forth through the swinging door that connected our kitchen and dining room, depending on which provided better shelter. You wouldn't believe how far a phone cord can stretch when you are truly desperate.

When we went to friends' houses or somewhere after school, we didn't have cell phones we could use to call our parents, or ones that they could use to track us down. "Then how did your mom and dad know where you were all the time?" Abe once asked. "They didn't," I said. "And it was wonderful!"

Back then we actually talked to each other instead of texting. We also answered the phone whenever it rang, because we didn't have Caller ID, Call Waiting, or anything else that gave us the luxury of prioritizing our personal phone calls. The only call we could accurately predict was the one we got *every* night at six o'clock from my grandfather. It was like clockwork. Just as we would sit down for dinner, the phone would ring, and all five of us would chant in harmony, "It's Paaaaapa!" We then started the original game of phone tag—passing a corded phone from one person to another until it finally got to the right one. Our nightly games of phone tag during dinner would start with my mother, who sat closest to the wall phone in the kitchen, and the phone would be passed from kid to kid until it got to my father. We then spent the first few minutes of our meal eating in silence, with a long, white phone cord stretched under our chins across the table.

I now read news stories about teenagers with tendonitis from texting too much, hear of calamities and car crashes blamed on calling and texting while driving, and see daily evidence that this technology isn't just a modern convenience—it's a modern addiction. Frankly, it's an addiction that Alan and I hope to keep from our own children as long as we can. Of course, we also know this rite of passage is inevitable, and it's only a matter of time before all three of our children have their own cell phones. That means by the time Arthur really wants to have "the talk," I'll be able to text him all about it.

CHAPTER FIVE

Am I There Yet?

The Guy's Perfect Spouse

MY FATHER RECENTLY BOUGHT A NEW CAR. THIS MIGHT BE A ROUTINE event in most people's lives, but for my father, it was a momentous occasion. You see, my father does not buy new cars. He buys *used* cars that are in exceptional condition. And he only does this when (a) one of his used cars has been driven beyond use; or (b) someone in the family totals a car. In this case, it was the latter. And even though my mother was the unfortunate victim of this collision, and she will want me to add that it was not her fault, my father was the one who benefited. He bought a new car, and he is the one now driving it. Or, rather, the car is now driving him.

Besides having all the state-of-the-art technologies you'd expect in a new car, like the built-in DVD player, heated seats, and satellite radio system, my dad's new ride is also equipped with a GPS. Most people assume GPS stands for Global Positioning System, a navigational tool that uses specially coded satellite signals to compute position, velocity, and time. I, on the other hand, refer to this system as the Guy's Perfect Spouse.

The Guy's Perfect Spouse is the most intuitive, composed woman I have ever met. You tell her where you need to go, and she immediately figures out the quickest route and leads you there—not just most of the time, but every time. Her sultry, calming voice is unwavering; she never loses her cool, never gets frustrated, and never talks back. Even when you miss a turn, she quickly computes a new route and, in her all-forgiving manner, redirects you to your destination. In fact, GPS regularly does what no other woman on earth has ever been able to accomplish—she successfully tells men where to drive.

My father is a fanatic when it comes to directions. Whenever he gets or gives directions, he doesn't just note turns or street names; he lists exact mileage and specific landmarks. He has even been known to test-drive a route days before he actually needs to take it. He has a self-proclaimed "impeccable sense of direction"—and, like most men, he would rather be lost for days than ask directions from a stranger, or even his own wife.

So you can imagine my surprise when my father introduced me to the new woman in his life—the GPS. At the time, we were in Atlanta for a family gathering, and we wanted to see our cousin's new home. It was no shocker that Dad wanted to drive, but I almost fell out of the car when he told me he didn't know how to get there and he hadn't even called ahead for directions. He was leaving it up to "her."

As we drove to my cousin's house, our conversation was intermittently interrupted by GPS's casual prompts and clear-cut directions. Dad never questioned her authority, never hesitated at a turn, and never second-guessed her suggestions. It was weird, like something on *The Twilight Zone*. My mother was away on business, and I wondered, "Does Mom know about this? About 'her'?"

We made it to my cousin's house without a hitch, and a few hours later we were headed back to the hotel. The return trip was equally effortless, and Dad glowed with satisfaction.

Just as I was about to praise the Guy's Perfect Spouse as the consummate navigator and the perfect driving companion, it happened—she and my father had their first fight. She prompted him to take a left turn, and Dad exclaimed, "What? That can't be right!"

I looked at him in disbelief. Was he now questioning the all-knowing GPS? She gave him a second warning, again directing him to turn. Dad just shook his head. "No, no, that's wrong," he said. "She doesn't know what she's talking about."

At this point I felt uncomfortable. I offered to leave the car for a few minutes while the two of them worked this out. But Dad didn't seem to hear me. In fact, he didn't seem to hear either one of us. He ignored me *and* the GPS and went his own way, which indeed turned out to be the wrong way. And as hard as it was for Dad to admit that the GPS was right, I knew it would be harder for him to accept that the GPS would never be wrong.

The fact is, while the GPS might be a Guy's Perfect Spouse, my father already had one of his own. And even though his new car was pretty cool, he definitely missed his old navigation system—my mother.

Friday Night Live

I WOULD LIKE TO BE ON *SATURDAY NIGHT LIVE* ONE DAY. NOT BECAUSE I THINK I am particularly funny, but because I would like to be the person who yells out, "Live from New York, it's Saturday night!" Just once. That's all I need.

I love Saturday nights. In fact, I think there is something quite magical and exciting about them. That's because when I was growing up, Saturday night was the only night of the week I was allowed to go out, my only night of freedom. Sunday through Thursday were school nights, so of course going out anywhere, unless it was to a friend's house to "study," was completely out of the question. And Friday night is the Jewish Sabbath. And God forbid I got out on the Sabbath—literally.

I grew up in a Conservative Jewish home, and every Friday night, my siblings and I were chained kicking and screaming to the dining room table, forced to recite Hebrew prayers and hang out with our grandparents. It was a tortuous ritual, especially considering all our friends were at the movies or the mall or high school football games, experiencing the proper rites of passage. While they were having the time of their teenage lives, we were eating brisket and listening to our grandfather belch.

Every so often there would be a really important occasion, like a friend's sleepover or a Prince concert, and my parents would grant us a temporary reprieve. But we still had to wait until *after* dinner before we could go out.

Life was so unfair.

The good news was that we were allowed to invite people to spend the night on Friday nights, which made the entire evening more palatable, at least. Of course, when word got out to the general teenage population that spending Friday night at the Goldstein house required a minimum of praying and dinner with the entire extended family, we became social outcasts. Even the Jewish kids started avoiding our calls. There is nothing worse than being shunned by members of your own tribe.

My parents said they were doing this for our own good. (Yeah, right. Like we hadn't heard *that* before.) They said family time was important, and that one day we would appreciate them for doing this. I said I would *never* do this to my own kids. But during all those years of eating my mother's cooking, I never imagined that one day, I would be eating my own words.

It has taken me a husband, three children, and nearly forty years to realize the method to my parents' madness, but I finally appreciate the virtue of the Friday night dinner. First of all, no matter how hectic our week has been or our weekend plans may be, we can always count on being together as a family every Friday night. Secondly, no matter how many times we eat out or order in, my family can always count on a home-cooked meal at least once a week.

Alan and I have discussed how important this tradition is for our family and that our children will have to understand this decision, and more importantly, live by it. And I'm sure that when they are teenagers, we will be having the same arguments with them as I had with my own parents. But luckily they will be given the same reprieves for special occasions—and Prince concerts.

A few years ago, we took our sons to Birmingham to visit my parents. Friday night dinner was almost exactly as I remembered it—my aunt and uncle sat at one end of the table, my ninety-one-year-old grandmother was in her usual place, and my mom's brisket had never smelled better. The only things missing were my siblings and my grandfather's belching.

Right before we sat down to eat, one of my best friends from high school called to see if I could go out that night. Without hesitation, I said, "Sure, but I can't go out until after dinner." Then I sat down and listened as our children led us in the Hebrew prayers, and I smiled, realizing that what I used to consider a sacrifice had become a sacred ritual—that during all those years of "missing out," I had really gained so much.

I looked around the table at my parents and the rest of my family, and for the first time in my life, I wanted to tell the world how happy I was to be there. So I stood up, pushed my chair back, and yelled, "Live from Alabama, it's Friday night!"

Ad Nauseam

WHEN I WAS A KID, I ABSOLUTELY LOVED TELEVISION COMMERCIALS. Those catchy jingles and infectious phrases were all part of my childhood vernacular. I wished I were an Oscar Mayer Wiener, I took the Pepsi Challenge and then had a Coke and a smile, I knew how to order two all-beef patties, special sauce, lettuce, cheese, pickles, onions on a sesame seed bun and to ask, "Where's the beef?" And I never *once* squeezed the Charmin. The influence all that useless information had on my life was irrefutable, and now that I am a mother, that's exactly why I absolutely abhor advertisements.

If you've ever watched children's television, you're aware of the ridiculous ratio of commercials to programming. I'm not really sure whether the commercials are supposed to provide a break from the programs, or the programs from the clutter of commercials. And I have tried to explain to our three boys that advertisements have only one purpose—to sell you something. I constantly remind them that toys do not really come to life when you play with them, soda does not really give you a burst of energy, and as far as I know, it has never once rained Skittles.

One afternoon, while the boys were watching television (and I, of course, was in the kitchen cooking a healthy and well-balanced meal) the "three-Mom fire alarm" went off. This is when at least one and usually all three of the boys yell, "MOM! MOM! MOM!" so urgently that, with Pavlovian instinct, I drop whatever I'm doing and run to see who is hurt or, even worse, who has spilled fruit punch on the couch again.

As I hurried into the den, the boys frantically asked, "How old are you? How old are you?" A little confused, I answered, "I'm thirty-eight. Why do you ask?" A crestfallen look came over their little faces, and finally Abe responded with a deep sigh, "Never mind. You have to be eighteen to buy this product." I started to explain what that really meant, until I realized my good fortune in this misunderstanding and merely said, "Oh, well," and went on my way.

But television commercials and my professional marketing background have at least taught me a valuable parenting skill: the art of creating the commercial child. This is the model of good behavior and politeness we prefer to take to restaurants, introduce to our colleagues, and brag about to our friends and family. This child bears absolutely no resemblance to the one who throws a tantrum when he gets frustrated, puts his brother in a headlock just for fun, or picks his nose while sucking his thumb. This is the public persona we parents can be proud of.

So a few weeks ago, when a friend asked if our boys would like to be in a print ad for a local museum, the proud mother in me immediately accepted, while the PR professional in me knew this was a potential crisis situation. The day of the shoot, the boys were pictures of perfection in their coordinating polo shirts. On the way to the museum, we went over the rules of engagement, and for good measure I told them we'd visit the ice cream shop if all went well. After all, every good actor needs some sort of motivation.

Much to my relief and surprise, they were the dream team. For that one hour, they sat where they were supposed to sit, smiled when they were supposed to smile, and never once touched each other—or their noses, for that matter. It was an award-winning performance, to say the least.

In fact, it was such a convincing performance that as we sat down for our ice cream, I started thinking maybe this was for real. Maybe they had finally seen the light and understood that good behavior would reap them even better benefits. Maybe my children weren't just acting; maybe this was how my children really act. But as soon as that thought crossed my mind, one of the boys kicked the other under the table, and the third punched the first, just to get some skin in the game. Still, when I eventually ushered them out of the ice cream shop and into the car, I was smiling, because all I could think of was that old Chiffon margarine commercial: "It's not nice to fool Mother Nature."

Doing It All

P ARENTS ARE EXPECTED TO DO A LOT OF THINGS FOR THEIR CHILDREN, BUT let's face it—moms are expected to do *every*thing. And we are expected to do them exceedingly well and without question or complaint. This isn't meant as a personal affront to my husband, or to any dads out there or grandparents or uncles or aunts or anyone else who has the responsibility of raising a child these days. And it is not intended to be some feminist declaration about the state of womanhood. It's just a somewhat obvious epiphany I recently had in the car rider line at school.

It was a Tuesday, and while I was driving my kids to school, they were excitedly discussing a special program that was taking place there that Thursday night. It suddenly dawned on me that I had double-booked my calendar, having committed to an important meeting that same evening. I apologetically admitted that I wasn't sure I was going to make it to the school event.

"What?" said my six-year-old, irately. "You won't be there? You know, you are NOT being a very good mom these days. This is the second thing you have missed in a month!"

Levi was referring to the annual holiday lunch at school, which I had also double-booked by agreeing to chaperone a field trip for our fifth-grader the same day. But even though his words were just the typical, visceral reaction of a disappointed child, they also really hurt my feelings. "I'm not a bad mom," I thought. "I'm just a poor scheduler." At this point I was pulling up to the school, and so with little time to respond rationally or make my case, I simply replied, "You know, I'm only one person. I can't do it all." And as Levi jumped out of the car and headed up the stairs to school, his parting words to me were, "Yes you can, Mom!"

I then felt bearing down on my own shoulders the weight borne by my mother, and by generations of "do-it-all mothers" before me. I had signed up for a job that has no rule book, but for which there is a single Golden Rule that all mothers must obey: *Thou shalt do it all.*

Our children's role is not to give us welcoming words of encouragement, daily doses of appreciation, or casual kudos on our hard work. That's what our spouses and therapists are for. Our children are there to keep us on our toes, to set impossible expectations they have no doubt we can achieve, and to inspire us to sync our iPhones with our husbands' BlackBerries so things like double-booking can be avoided at all costs.

I drove home a bit dismayed, thinking about all the things my mother used to do for her family, and still does, without pause or praise. She maintained what was no doubt a precarious balance of work and home, of wife and mother, with the utmost grace and gratitude. She was like Betty Crocker, Gloria Steinem, and Mary Tyler Moore all rolled up in one. To this day, when she walks into a room, I swear I can hear that old commercial for Enjoli perfume playing in the background—"I can bring home the bacon, da da da dum ... "

And of course, all the things I came to expect automatically as a child I can now fully appreciate as a mom. Because there is only one person on this earth who will chew second-hand gum when her child can't find a trash can, who will untie knotted shoelaces with her teeth without once considering where those shoes have been, and who can always figure out a way to be two places at one time. That's why tough guys get the word *Mom* tattooed on their arms, why football players instinctively yell, "Hi, Mom!" into every television camera, and why a child who's sitting in the kitchen right next to his dad will still yell across the house to ask his mom for a glass of milk.

Unfortunately, this revelation did nothing to help rectify my immediate situation and the double-booking. But luckily, the weather did. Two days later it snowed, school was cancelled, and the school program was postponed until the following month. And Levi was right all along—I was able to do it all.

Snow Business

T HERE IS NOTHING THAT TESTS THE LIMITS OF A FAMILY BETTER THAN A
snowstorm—especially in the South, where even the threat of a snowfall
triggers the same sort of panic and preparation most Americans would
associate with a Cold War-era threat of nuclear attack. Except instead of bomb
shelters filled with canned goods, southerners have basements filled with
cheap sleds.

Well before the first snowflake hits the ground, we hit the ground running,
feverishly scrounging for the basic necessities—milk, eggs, and Kraft Macaroni
& Cheese. Even those of us who normally don't eat eggs feel compelled to buy
at least a dozen, just in case. We then travel to every Walmart, Target, and
sporting goods store within a twenty-mile radius in hopes of finding waterproof
clothing, plastic toboggans, and WD-40, which we believe we will need after
we transform the modest hill in front of our house into an Olympic-worthy
luge track using only a plastic shovel and two inches of powder.

Of course, most of the time, our preparation is in vain. In the South, big
promises of heavy snow usually amount to little more than the premature
closing of schools and a light dusting that disappears by daybreak. But every
so often, that Doppler radar does right by us and we get a downright dumping.
And it's doggone delightful … for a day.

Yes, that first day is magical. Schools and offices are closed, and people pour
into the streets with their dogs and children. There are snowball fights, sledding,
and snowmen all over the city, and all before breakfast. At lunchtime we bring
homemade soups and fresh produce to our neighbors' home for a potluck meal
and a friendly game of poker, surrounded by friends. We reminisce about the
snowstorms of yesteryear as the white wonderland outside somehow makes
the whole world seem merry and happy and bright.

Day two is not so cheerful. Schools and offices are still closed, and in
between sledding and hot cocoa breaks, we strategically shovel our sidewalks
and driveways in hopes of maneuvering our two-wheel-drive minivans out
of our garages. The eggs we purchased actually come in handy at the potluck
neighborhood brunch, but instead of betting hands at poker, we now sit
around betting when school will ever be back in session. We also wonder when
that white stuff will ever melt and when our kids will ever tire of playing in it.

Day three and beyond are just plain dreadful. What started as family
bonding has quickly deteriorated into family bondage. We parents are texting
anyone we know who has a four-wheel drive, hoping they can pick us up or, at
the very least, drop off a babysitter. We no longer arrange neighborhood meals,

because we are now hoarding whatever food we have left and wondering why we bought milk but not toilet paper when we had the chance. And when the kids ask if we can have family poker night, we tell them all bets are off—and aren't they sick of sledding and building snowmen yet? To which they always reply with enthusiasm, "No way, this is awesome!"

That's when it occurs to us that maybe all those wonderful memories we have about that "big snowstorm" when we were kids are not the same memories our parents have.

For instance, I fondly remember the time in 1980 when there was a blizzard in Alabama and Mom cooked all our meals on the outside grill and it was just like camping but we never had to leave our home and we all had a blast. Mom, however, remembers that time as the week Dad was stranded at a business meeting at the Ritz Carlton in Atlanta while she was stranded with three brats and a crazy dog in a house that had no power so she was forced to cook the entire freezer of defrosted food on the gas grill outside in twenty-degree weather.

I am just thankful Mom finally got that off her chest.

The forecast this week calls for snow on Tuesday night, and the boys are already asking if school will be cancelled on Wednesday. To be safe, I have stocked up on milk, eggs, Kraft Macaroni & Cheese, and toilet paper. And I have left a forwarding number where my family can reach me.

At the Ritz.

Diagnosis: Google

I AM SITTING IN BED RIGHT NOW WITH A SEVERE CASE OF LARYNGITIS. MY throat is killing me, my ears are throbbing, and it is taking all my energy just to swallow. So I am doing what any responsible, intelligent mother of three would do in my situation: I am frantically searching the Internet for a cure.

I mean, seriously, who needs a real MD when I have thousands of virtual ones at the touch of a button? I could be gargling, but instead I am Googling, and I am really making progress. After browsing the first page of a possible 1,020,000 hits on laryngitis, I have learned that "it is usually caused by a virus or occurs in people who overuse their voice." And either I have "developed this from a bacterial infection" or, less likely, I have "tuberculosis, syphilis, or a fungal infection."

Great. That narrows it down.

After focusing my search on "laryngitis remedies," I get a mere 186,000 hits. The good news is that within these are multiple sites offering suggestions for home remedies. Now we're getting somewhere. At this rate, not only can I get medical advice from the comfort of home, but I may never have to leave my house again for medical treatment, either. After reading through a few of these natural cures, I am pretty sure that some hot tea with a mixture of cayenne pepper, apple cider vinegar, onion syrup, honey, and lemon will do the trick. It doesn't really say to mix all of these together, but I figure if each ingredient is effective alone, then combining them should certainly expedite my recovery.

Okay, the real problem, if you must know—besides the fact that I may or may not have some rare, terminal disease and that I am out of cayenne pepper—is that I do not have a doctor. Let me rephrase that—I do not have a "primary care physician." I realized this about a year ago, when I was suffering from a similar ailment and was self-diagnosed with strep throat. I called my OB-GYN's office and left a message for the nurse, asking her to please phone in a simple Z-Pak to my local pharmacy. She called me back, and the following conversation ensued:

> **Nurse:** I understand you have a very bad sore throat.
> **Me:** *struggling to talk.* Yes, it's killing me.
> **Nurse:** I see. Well, are you currently pregnant or breast-feeding?
> **Me:** *struggling to comprehend her question.* Um, no.
> **Nurse:** Then I am really sorry. I cannot help you. You will have to call your primary care physician for that.

Me:	Okay, but I thought you *were* my primary care physician. The only other doctor I go to on a regular basis is my dentist.
Nurse:	I am very sorry.
Me:	Wait, what if I promise to try and get pregnant tonight— then will you call me in a prescription?
Nurse:	I am really sorry. *click.*

What I want to know is, what happened to the good ol' one-stop-shop physician that existed when I was a kid? When my children need to see a doctor, it's simple—they go to their pediatrician. For my complex adult ailments, however, I need an ENT, an OB-GYN, and a slew of other letter combinations just to cover the basics. I'm calling the AMA about this MD issue ASAP!

I think doctors' offices should be more like Target. They should have great customer service, address all my needs in one place, and take American Express. No matter what I need, ninety-nine percent of the time I can end up finding it at Target. Books, pillows, batteries, salad tongs? Target. Target. Target. Target. Is it too much to ask that my healthcare be just as convenient, not to mention affordable?

It's not like I'm asking to get a throat culture, Pap smear, and teeth cleaning at the same time—although that would be pretty awesome. I just want the luxury of going to one doctor when I am sick or healthy or pregnant or not and have that doctor be able to diagnose and treat me and send me on my way with a smile and a lollipop. And if that's too much to ask, then I guess that leaves me with only one option: I'm waking up my husband and telling him I need to get pregnant tonight. This tea is really awful.

Pillow Talk

I F I HAD TO PINPOINT THE SINGLE MOST RIDICULOUS ONGOING POINT OF contention in my marriage, I could do it in just two words: show pillows.

For those of you who are wondering what a show pillow is, let me offer two standard definitions. The "female" definition of a show pillow is "a decorative addition to any bed, which creates aesthetic value and beauty." The "male" definition of a show pillow is "a stupid addition to any bed, which offers no value or purpose."

Admittedly, a show pillow serves no utilitarian function. One would never dare *use* a show pillow. That's why they're called "show" pillows—they're only for show. If they were meant to be used, they would be, well, pillows.

Anyway, a few years ago and a few weeks before Alan's birthday, he casually said one night, "I know what I want for my birthday." I was eager to hear the answer, since I never know what to get the guy. "I want you to get the show pillows off the bed," he said. "I can't stand them."

I just laughed and thought, "Yeah, right. And let's just take all the shades off the lamps and the legs off the tables and the seats off the toilets." And then I thought, "Oh wait, he'd probably like that last one."

Unfortunately, he was serious, and this was no show. We ultimately reached a compromise: I agreed to remove the show pillows during the normal course of life, and he agreed to let me put them back on the bed under special circumstances or in an emergency situation—like when we had guests, or when my parents came to visit.

So for years now, those show pillows have taken up permanent residence in my closet. But a few weeks ago, they finally got their long-awaited freedom. It was a Saturday, and our three boys were spending the night at their grandparents' house, so by 4:00 p.m. Alan and I had the house all to ourselves. Our plan was to meet some friends out somewhere, until Alan suggested that our friends come over to our house, instead. I stared at my disheveled domicile in disbelief and then panicked, realizing I had less than an hour to turn my mess into a masterpiece. And that's when the frenzy began.

My house might look like a disaster area on occasion, but give me sixty minutes and I can turn even the most pathetic dump pristine. I come by it honestly; I am a second-generation frenzied fixer-upper. I inherited this skill from my mother, who can still put an otherwise disastrous room in order in ten minutes flat.

The problem is, I have a penchant for piling things around my house. In the kitchen, the living room, my office, our bedroom, you name it—give me a flat surface, and I will give it a pile of stuff. But with the threat of outsiders entering our abode, I became a typhoon of tidiness. With a spray bottle in one hand and a trash bag in the other, I was folding and tucking and dusting and cleaning, and, most of all, hiding the evidence of my daily life.

Alan looked on with what I thought was awe, when in fact it was more like annoyance. "What are you doing?" he asked. "The house looks great. You don't have to make it look perfect."

Of course I had to make the house look perfect! The advantage of having guests over is that these people don't live with me and have no idea how my house normally looks. So I ignored his remarks and asked him to please clear his own piles off the living room chair. He rolled his eyes but ultimately gave in.

After the last pile was neatly hidden in my laundry room, the final game piece thrown into the closet, and all the messy remnants of our lives safely stowed, it was time for the finishing touch: the show pillows.

I took the five bulky beauties out of my closet, dusted them off, and said, "It's showtime, ladies!" I then placed them strategically on our bed. As I took a step back to admire my hard work, Alan came into the room, carrying his pile from the living room chair.

"So, what do you think?" I asked.

He stared at the pillows, shook his head, and replied, "It's very clean, but it doesn't look like anyone lives here!"

I took a deep breath, smiled, and said, "Thank you, Honey. That's the nicest thing you've ever said."

Fright of Passage

A FTER MY SIBLINGS AND I WERE ALL MARRIED, MY MOTHER SPENT THE next few years longing for that phone call—the one that would convey those four little words she was dying to hear: "We're having a baby!" Now, nine grandchildren later, it was only a matter of time before one of them called to share those four little words my mother never wanted to hear: "Nini, I'm playing football."

"I'm sorry, what did you say?" my mother said worriedly into the phone, as our oldest son, Arthur, excitedly told her the news.

"I'm playing football, Nini!" he repeated. "Isn't that awesome?"

"Football? But isn't that the sport where they knock you down and beat you up? What happened to tennis, Honey?"

By now, Arthur had handed the phone to me, and I had to calmly explain to my mother that yes, it was true: her precious progeny would soon be passing the pigskin.

To be fair, this was a unilateral decision in my household—made by my husband, Alan. It's not that I am against football. In elementary school I was actually one of the only girls who would play co-ed touch football during recess, and I was a pretty fierce competitor. But with Arthur, we were talking the real deal—full pads, mouth guard, tackles, and all. As the mother of three boys, I should have known this moment was inevitable, but as the daughter of a mother who constantly worries, I, too, had secretly hoped this day would never come.

Alan played football when he was in elementary school, and the stories of his triumphs and the days when he was known as "Crazy Legs" are legendary in our home. He had insisted that football is a rite of passage and would be good for Arthur. "It's a great team sport," Alan had said. "It will help build his endurance and his confidence, and it will make him into a man."

It will make him into a man? He's only ten. Can't that wait until his bar mitzvah?

The football season started out just as tough and traumatic as I had feared— the struggles, the agony, the tears—and that was just a trip to the sporting goods store to buy a helmet. I could only imagine what a day on the field would be like.

Football practices were grueling and consisted of drills that I can only compare to boot camp. After each practice, Arthur came home with a new set of bruises, which gave him immediate street cred with his two brothers. Each week, as they oohed and aahed at the sight of Arthur's black and blue marks, I would close my eyes, click my heels, and repeat, "There's no sport like tennis, there's no sport like tennis … "

But from the first game, I was comforted by the stands full of other anxious parents, who were as much a support group as a cheering section. And even though our team wasn't exactly the best in the league, I was constantly inspired by the obvious camaraderie among the boys and the sense of accomplishment they felt after every small success or completed play on the field. Even after a big loss, Arthur was always positive, recounting the times when he and his teammates really shined, and always adding, "It's okay, we'll get 'em next time."

The last game was here before we knew it, and it was the perfect way to end the season—a total shutout. As soon as Arthur got into the car, he knew exactly whom he wanted to call.

"Nini, guess what?" he shouted into the phone. "We won twenty-two to zero!"

"Baby Doll, I am so proud of you!" Mom exclaimed.

"Nini," Arthur said, "I am not a Baby Doll."

"Well, how about my Sweetie Pie?"

"No, not Sweetie Pie, either."

"Well if you're not my Baby Doll and you're not my Sweetie Pie," she said, "then what are you?"

Arthur answered with those four little words my husband couldn't wait to hear: "Nini, I'm a man."

Looks like we won't have to wait for his bar mitzvah, after all.

Smooth Move

NOW THAT I HAVE MORE THAN TEN YEARS OF PARENTING EXPERIENCE and three kids under my belt, I have come to a profound realization: dating would have been so much easier if I had raised three boys beforehand.

This dawned on me the other day when Arthur, our oldest son, had two of his friends over. When I went to the basement to check on them, I must have paused for a second too long, because all three gave me this *look*, and Arthur politely asked if I would mind leaving, since they wanted to talk privately.

As a mother who wants to give her boys the space they need, my instinct was to honor his request. But as a woman dying to know what fifth-grade boys actually talk about, I found myself glued to my seat.

"So, what's the topic?" I asked. They glanced at each other uncomfortably and merely answered, "Stuff." As if that would deter me.

"Well, what kind of stuff? I might be able to offer some insight," I said.

After some nervous laughter, one finally broke the unspoken boy code of silence and admitted, "Girls. We're talking about girls."

I managed to stifle my own laugh and said, "Well, then, I think I can be especially helpful, because we moms have the inside scoop when it comes to girls. That's because there is a tightly kept secret about us that I would be willing to share."

Their eyes grew wide and they each leaned forward, eager to hear what it was.

In a very dramatic whisper, I said, "What you may not know is that we moms are actually ... GIRLS!" Of course, this was news to them.

It turns out they had really only one question in mind: "If you decide you like a girl, then what's the next move?" All the boys awaited my response, eyeing me with newfound interest and attention.

So I asked the obvious: "What's your objective?" Before you can determine what to do, I explained, you need to figure out what you ultimately want.

"That doesn't matter," one of the boys said. "We just need to know the next move."

And that's when I realized that I had apparently wasted countless hours, weeks, and months analyzing and dissecting every romantic relationship or potential relationship in my life. My formative years were founded on the premise that every potential partner had a master plan, and now I was learning that nothing could have been further from the truth. While girls are strategizing and agonizing, contemplating and deliberating, boys evidently are thinking only one thing—"What's my next move?"

Let's put this in practical terms. When a girl goes on a first date with a boy, as soon as they sit down at a restaurant, she immediately begins thinking, "Could this be the right man for me? Does he want a big wedding or a small one? What will our children look like?" Meanwhile, the boy is thinking, "Should I have the steak or the chicken?"

As I sat pondering this epiphany, I noticed the boys still huddled around me in eager anticipation. "So, what's the next move?" one of them repeated anxiously.

I started by saying I didn't think fifth-graders should even *have* moves—that they were too young to date or go steady or whatever the term is these days, and that friendship was complicated enough without creating these mature labels. I also acknowledged that their feelings were totally natural and that I was proud of them for being so open and honest.

I then noticed the gleam in their eyes starting to fade, so, fearing they might lose all faith in the female perspective, I rebounded with the only move I could think of: "So, your next move should be to head to the kitchen for some lemonade and popcorn!" And they all cheered and ran up the stairs.

As a girl, I may never understand what boys are thinking. But as a mom, I always know what makes them happy.

Who's Sorry Now?

WHY IS IT SO EASY FOR US TO MAKE MISTAKES AND YET SO DIFFICULT for us to render apologies? I'm not talking about the lackadaisical, less-than-legitimate kind of apology most people give while saying it in passing— "Oh … sorry." Or the angry, accusatory apology—"Well, SORRY!"—that makes it sound like it's actually the other person's fault. And don't even get me started on the sarcastic, "Sorry, Charlie" sort of apology made famous in those StarKist Tuna ads and used so flippantly by all the other fish in the sea. Because no matter how you say it, spray it, or try to play it, there is nothing sorrier than a sub-par sorry.

So when my friend Jill shared her concept of the three-step apology, I was just sorry I hadn't thought of it myself. She came up with the idea after listening to a portion of *The Last Lecture*, the now-famous speech and book by Carnegie Mellon professor Randy Pausch, who wrote it as a legacy to his children before he passed away. This part, in particular, dealt with apologies; basically, Pausch said a bad apology is worse than no apology at all. He went on to speak about how apologizing is one of the most important skills we can learn. The proper apology, he said, has three parts: *What I did was wrong. I feel badly that I hurt you. How do I make you feel better?*

An educator herself, Jill was inspired by this new way of thinking and came up with her own version of the three-part apology to use in the classroom: *I'm sorry. I take full responsibility. How can I make it up to you?* The first time Jill put this philosophy into practice, she was amazed at the results. After a longtime bully belittled a smaller boy in front of some of their classmates, Jill insisted that the bully deliver this three-part apology to his victim, who was not only hurt but also deeply embarrassed. After the bully complied, the smaller boy looked him in the eye and said, "There is nothing you can ever do to make this up to me," and walked away. The bully cried his eyes out, at which point Jill said to him, "I believe that is consequence enough." Since that day, she reports, that boy has never bullied another person again.

So Alan and I decided to implement Jill's three-part apology in our own household, and the results have been equally stunning. When one of our sons does something wrong and then apologizes for it, he knows that a plain "sorry" won't cut it; instead, he will launch into the *I'm sorry. I take full responsibility. How can I make it up to you?* mantra. The only thing better than hearing those words come out of the boys' mouths—hearing them accept responsibility for their actions in such a profound way—is listening to the creative responses they give for how the perpetrator can "make it up."

I think you should lose your Nintendo DS for a month.
I think you should make my bed for a week.
I think you should have to sit in complete silence at the dinner table tonight.
I think you should give me all your Level X Pokémon cards.
I think you should never, ever do that again.

Even though some of these suggestions don't get implemented, I always give props to the boys for their creativity and resourcefulness. And in our house, no one is immune. A few months ago when I wrongly accused Abe of doing something and then simply said, "Sorry," he looked me in the eye and said, "That's not a real apology, Mom. I need to hear the three steps."

And he was right. So I stopped what I was doing and instead responded, "Honey, I am so sorry for accusing you and making you feel bad. I take full responsibility. How can I make it up to you?" Abe thought long and hard before saying, "That's okay, Mom, I know you didn't mean it. Just don't do it again." And before walking away, he added, "I still love you."

And for me, that was consequence enough.

Nothing but the Truth

ONE OF THE BEST THINGS ABOUT MY HUSBAND, ALAN, IS THAT HE IS THE most truthful person I know. And this has proven to be quite an asset in our marriage ... most of the time. That's because as much as I love an honest man, any honest woman will tell you that she doesn't always want to hear the truth. Especially when it comes to that age-old question, "Honey, how do I look?"

Let me state the obvious here: when a woman asks a man how she looks, it's a total setup, a no-win situation. We both know that. And when she asks it, the man has three options. He can (a) tell her what she wants to hear, that she looks gorgeous and skinny; (b) tell her what he really thinks and then suffer the consequences; or (c) pretend to be on his BlackBerry and avoid the question altogether.

Alas, my husband has often chosen to respond with what he believes to be the no-fail, safe answer, option (d) tell her that she looks "cute." For the record, telling a woman she looks cute is basically the kiss of death. I would rather my husband tell me I look like a fat, drowned rat than tell me I look cute. Well, not really, but you get the point.

For a while, Alan and I had an understood "Don't ask, don't tell" policy about this. That's because besides being brutally honest, he also happens to be a terrible liar. So I didn't ask him how I looked, and he didn't tell me what he thought. This policy was actually the direct result of what we now refer to as "The Comment of 2000." When I was about seven months pregnant with our first son and getting more pregnant by the hour, I turned to my husband one day and asked, "Do you think my butt has gotten bigger?" To which he immediately replied, "Nope, not at all." To which I tearfully responded, "You mean my butt is ALWAYS this big?" As I said before—total setup.

But after a few years of relying on my own judgment and on department store mirrors, which are totally rigged to make you look skinnier, I made a critical decision—I really did want to know what Alan thought. So I started to ask, and he was actually a pretty reliable source. "I like the first dress better than the second," he would offer. "I wouldn't wear that jacket, it's too dressy," or, "Those earrings are too big. Wear the dangly ones."

Lately, though, his truthful tendencies have gone a little too far. These days he doesn't even wait for me to ask before he offers his opinion.

The last straw was when I bought a series of dresses that all got the thumbs-down. I finally found a simple black dress that I knew was just perfect, but when I tried it on, Alan immediately gave me that "look." My delight dissolved into disappointment.

"What, you don't like it?" I asked.

"No, I don't. It looks terrible on you," he began. "It drapes too much, and it's not at all flattering … Who told you it looked good, anyway?"

That's when I realized that even though I do care what my husband thinks, I don't always care to hear it. But just as I was about to stomp off, hurt and insulted, he added, "Honey, it's like telling you that you have spinach in your teeth. I'm doing you a favor." And in a funny way, he was.

So I decided to pull a George Costanza—borrowed straight from the eighty-sixth episode of *Seinfeld*. If all of my instincts had been so wrong, then I would start doing the opposite of what I would instinctively do. Instead of getting defensive, I thanked him. Instead of keeping the dress in spite of him, I returned it the very next day. Then I bought a sexy black number that was a little shorter and more form-fitting than I would typically wear.

The next night I came into the living room for the big reveal, holding in my breath (and my stomach), and somewhat anxious about what he might say. I finally asked, "So, what do you think?" Alan looked up and said, "Wow, you look hot!"

At last, an honest answer that was also exactly what I wanted to hear.

Game Boys

About once a week, we try to have a family game night at our house, and let me tell you, there is nothing better than bonding over a good, old-fashioned board game. We are a bona fide board game family. You name it, we play it—from checkers and chess to Blokus and Battleship. We deal it, roll it, buy it, sell it, move it, lose it, applaud it, and curse it, all in the name of family fun. The image of the five of us eagerly gathered around the table, laughing and competing, would make the Parker Brothers proud.

But recently it occurred to me there was one game we had never played: the Game of LIFE. Our boys discovered this recreational relic at their cousins' house a few months ago and have been hooked on it ever since. According to Wikipedia (I live for Wikipedia), the Game of LIFE, also known simply as LIFE, was originally created by Milton Bradley in 1860 as the Checkered Game of Life. It simulates a person's travels through his or her life, from college to retirement, with jobs, marriages, and children (or not) along the way. A "modern" version was published one hundred years later, and updated as recently as 2005.

Ironically, I have never played any version of the game—and I grew up in a fairly devoted board game family. I guess I was more of a Candy Land girl, myself. And who could blame me? Who needs to graduate from college or pursue a career when you could live the sweet life atop Gumdrop Mountain or in the Candy Cane Forest?

The 1960s-era commercial proclaimed, "You will learn about life when you play the Game of LIFE." So one day last week, as I watched our three boys setting up the board game on our kitchen table, I decided to become an impartial observer and see if this claim was still true.

The best part of the game, for me, was that I did not have to read the directions. And believe me, they are intricate and confusing at best. Luckily, the boys learned most of the rules while playing with their older cousins, and they took turns reading what they didn't remember or couldn't agree upon along the way.

As I watched them play, I quickly saw that each boy fit into a distinct category: the rule-maker, the rule-breaker, and the rule-faker. Arthur, our oldest, was following the instructions to the letter, keeping his money in impeccable order, and generally playing the game in a manner befitting a descendant of Milton Bradley. Our middle son, Abe, had one and only one goal in mind: to make money. So what if he took a few extra spins, snagged a few extra dollars, and traded in a few children for a tax refund? He was in it to win it. Levi, our youngest, was playing a game of his own making. When he didn't agree with the rule at hand, he made up his own, and he somehow managed to land on Pay Day on every turn. If any of his self-made rules was contested, he would fight back—and usually win. In fact, he wore down his brothers to the point that eventually they gave up arguing with him altogether.

During the course of the game, I heard some classic conversations. Some of my favorite lines included ...

> *Hey, you can't sue me again.*
> *No way, I am NOT buying a house without a salary increase.*
> *Oh, cool, I almost had a baby boy!*
> *Yes, Mom, for the last time, we are ALL married.*

As I continued to watch them receive their college degrees, deliberate on their careers, buy their first homes, and earn their own salaries, it was enough to make any mom proud. And even though this was just a game, in a way it also was a fitting commentary on the boys' lives, or at least how I hope their lives will play out. I happily imagined them creating their own successful paths, achieving everything they set out to accomplish, and best of all, doing it together, as brothers, having fun and supporting each other along the way.

The game came to an end, and I quickly transitioned from being an innocent bystander to an independent banker when the boys begged me to count all their winnings. After each paid off more than a hundred thousand dollars in bank loans, I was happy to report that they were all successful millionaires. Abe "won" the game with more than three million dollars in hand (any accusations of embezzlement have yet to be proven) and decided to retire at the ripe old age of seven. I didn't have the heart to tell him that even with that kind of money in the bank, he would need a lot more to help sustain the home, wife, and children he had also acquired, and that he would probably be broke before his bar mitzvah. Instead, I helped the boys clean up the board and handed them a new game to play. It's called Sorry!

Aim Higher

OUR OLDEST SON, ARTHUR, IS REALLY INTO BASKETBALL THESE DAYS. Actually, he is really into sports in general. He reads the sports page every morning, turns on ESPN every night, and shares random sports facts and stats with anyone who will listen. So it should have come as no surprise to me when the other day, as he was shooting hoops in the driveway, Arthur turned to me and asked, "Mom, do you think I could play in the NBA someday?" And being the loving and supportive mom that I am, I looked him straight in the eye and said, "Nope."

Apparently this was not the one-word answer he was looking for. Crestfallen and on the verge of tears, he demanded to know why I would say such a mean thing. I told him I wasn't trying to be mean—just honest. I pointed out that he simply didn't put enough energy into the sport, and that practicing a couple of hours a week did not constitute a serious effort and would not get him into the pros.

To further prove my point, I asked, "Do you think you are as good at basketball as Daddy?" He shook his head. "And do you think Daddy is as good as an NBA player?" He reluctantly shook his head again. "Well, then, according to the transitive property, you are not as good as an NBA player, so there is your answer." I always knew the transitive property would come in handy one day.

Anyone will tell you that I am the eternal optimist, the hopeless romantic, and the ultimate dreamer. And yet for some reason, when it comes to my own children, instead of offering them a spoonful of sugar, I inject them with a healthy dose of reality. They want Mary Poppins, and I give them Dirty Harry. That's because the aspirational side of me that wants to assure my children they can do and be anything they want is balanced by the practical part of me that needs to protect them in the event that they don't.

When my husband came home from work that evening, Arthur immediately told on me. Fortunately, Alan was prepared with the perfect pep talk. He told Arthur that he could certainly achieve anything he wanted to, but only if he worked hard, stayed focused, and was willing to give it one hundred percent.

I told them that's exactly what I'd meant when I said, "Nope."

So Arthur dedicated every free moment of the next week to living, breathing, and sweating basketball. He even kept a detailed log of every minute he spent running drills, taking shots, and practicing his moves. By all indications, he had learned a valuable lesson. And, in the middle of that same week, I learned one as well.

Alan and I attended a fundraiser at which the keynote speaker was a woman named Bonnie St. John, who is, among other things, an author, life coach, and Olympic medalist in skiing. She also has just one leg. Bonnie talked about all the possibilities and opportunities she has had in her life—ones that certainly seemed to outweigh any challenges or barriers. She talked about dreaming big and living even bigger. And then she shared the story of a mother whose son had been terribly burned, and who asked Bonnie if the boy could ever hope to lead a normal life. Bonnie said she knew the mother wanted a simple, one-syllable response; she wanted to hear the word *yes*. But Bonnie couldn't give that to her. Instead, she looked the mother in the eye and said, "No. Aim higher. Aim higher."

After she spoke, I glanced at Alan and knew exactly what he was thinking. "I didn't give Arthur very good advice the other day, did I?" I asked, hoping for a response that would alleviate my guilt. But what Alan gave me was a one-syllable answer that sounded all too familiar—"Nope."

That evening, while tucking Arthur into bed, I told him how sorry I was for responding so abruptly and negatively to his question. I told him he could definitely play in the NBA, the NFL, or any of those acronyms someday, and that I wasn't there to crush or question his dreams, but instead to make sure he never gave up on them. And finally, I promised him that from now on, I would always aim higher. Just like he does.

Subtexting

I HAVE RECENTLY SOLVED THE AGE-OLD MYSTERY OF WHY MEN AND WOMEN have such a hard time communicating with each other. And it's all thanks to texting.

The beauty of texting is that it's a fast, efficient, and fantastic way to cram an entire conversation into a single line or simple acronym. This is also the downside of texting, as love notes, romantic cards, and phone calls all have been replaced by a few thumb clicks and four simple letters: LUV U. With all the LOLs, BTWs, and OMGs, reading a text message these days is about as easy as decoding a vanity license plate while driving 70 mph down the interstate.

It's also true that a response of "y" for "Yes" might be misconstrued for the question "Why?" and autocorrect insists on turning sentences like "Lots of people know him" into "Love to polka with Jim." But these are just minor speed bumps on the information superhighway.

The real source of any marital dispute, miscommunication, or minor disagreement is simple: men text, while women subtext. Men write what they think, and women veil how they feel. That explains why even the simplest text message written by a man will have an entirely different meaning and intention if written by a woman. Here's an example:

Man: What's for dinner tonight?

This man is obviously wondering what's for dinner tonight. Seems like a simple enough question. But let's take a look at a typical female response.

Woman: I don't know, what is for dinner tonight?

Now, a man would probably interpret her text as just a repetition of his original question. He might even think to himself, "Um, yeah, I just asked you the same question." Or possibly, "Well great, at least we're on the same page." Unfortunately, the man has missed the obvious subtext of this message. What the woman is really saying is, "Why are you asking me what's for dinner? I've been working all day and have spent the afternoon helping with homework and driving the kids to a million activities, and if you think I've had time to go to the grocery or even contemplate a meal, then you are sorely mistaken."

When a man finally interprets the subtext of her message, his response is always the same: "Why didn't you just say that in the first place?"

Men, of course, are supposed to know instinctively that a one-word response from a woman is actually code for a very complex, long-winded discussion she is having in her own mind. We women may not always text what we mean, but we always mean what we text, and we expect men to understand exactly what we're saying, even if we don't come out and say it. Is that too much to ask? We understand that men are literal, and that in a perfect world, women would be more direct, but let's face it, Moses was the one who talked to that burning bush. His sister Miriam would have just beaten around it.

During a recent conversation with our ten-year-old, I discovered that our sons are similarly clueless about subtexting. He wanted to know why I had such small wrists, and I told him they were there to balance out my wide hips and big booty. He didn't even crack a smile or question my response. Even worse, he failed to offer the one obligatory line that every woman expects at the mere implication that her posterior might be slightly plump—"You do *not* have a big butt."

But this concept of subtexting goes way beyond the old "Do I look fat in this outfit?" cat-and-mouse conversation. Subtexting is a way for women to test how well the men in their lives really know them. We don't expect them to be mind readers, but we do expect them to be superb subtext interpreters. So the next time a woman writes, "I'm fine," her partner should know she is anything but fine. The next time she texts, "What time will you be home?" I would suggest he get in the car immediately and stop by the grocery for a bouquet of tulips, just in case. And finally, when a woman says, "Honey, I have a headache," he should believe she actually means, "Honey, I have a headache." Yes, even with women, there are some texts that actually have no subtext at all.

LOL.

The Hands-On Mom

"HOLD MY HAND," I INSTRUCT MY BOYS WHEN WE CROSS THE STREET, with my arms outstretched as far as they will go. As the younger two instinctively grab hold, the oldest drifts farther away, saying, "I'm fine, I'm fine, I can cross by myself." While this is true, I grab his hand anyway and respond, "You might be able to cross the street by yourself, but just be thankful you don't have to!"

As our children get older, it seems that hand-holding is one of the first things to go—literally and figuratively. Kids start out as helpless little beings, dependent upon us for *everything*, and then somehow, right under our noses, they evolve into these independent, self-sufficient know-it-alls. It's a gradual transition, but somehow it still catches us off-guard.

During such moments I am reminded of the frequent road trips my family took when I was a kid, and how my mother would twist her arm awkwardly around her seat and reach toward the backseat, aimlessly fishing for one of our hands. When no one would take the bait, she would plead, "Hold my hand, please, for just a second." And like my own kids now, my siblings and I would just roll our eyes at each other and giggle at this pathetic plea for our affection. One of us would ultimately have to give in, usually the one sitting closest to her reach, but only for an instant, lest she get the wrong idea—that we *needed* to hold her hand, like we were still babies or something. Of course, in retrospect I realize that the hand-holding wasn't for our benefit. It was for hers.

I thought about this when Alan and I officially became parents of a child in the dreaded "double digits." At age ten, Arthur is nearly five feet tall, and his shoe size already equals his father's, so while he is still a few years away from puberty (we can only hope), this child is looking and acting more like a man each day.

So I am just grasping the concept of raising a true "tween" and, more importantly, learning how hard it is to be a "tween" myself—caught between the earnest desire to help my kids become independent, and the deeper impulse to protect and care for them, no matter how old they are. It's parental purgatory. For instance, while my husband thinks our eight-year-old is responsible enough to bike alone to a friend's house, he still doesn't trust our six-year-old to wipe himself. But what Alan categorizes as major milestones in our children's lives, I experience as tortuous turning points in my own. When Abe does bike to his friend's house, I pace the kitchen in agony, waiting for the phone to ring so I know he got there safely. My husband, on the other hand, sits calmly reading the newspaper, offering only a rhetorical, "What could possibly go wrong?"

What could possibly go wrong? He obviously has no clue about the complex workings of the female mind. I have at my disposal an endless list of worst-case scenarios that can be applied to any given situation involving any given person at any given time. The only thing that calms my nerves is speaking to friends who are even worse worry-mongers than I am. Like my friend Jill, who called the other day to say that Abe was ready to come home from playing at her house, but she was worried about him biking home—"you know, because of the coyote sightings in the area," she whispered into the phone. "And it will be dark soon."

I hopped in the car without hesitating.

When I was younger, I often wondered how old I would have to be before my parents finally stopped parenting me. When would they finally stop worrying whether I got somewhere in one piece? When would they finally stop asking how I was and if I needed anything?

The answer, of course, is never.

I now understand that the second a child comes into this world, a parent's internal clock of concern begins to tick, and it never stops. And while everyone will reassure you that, in many ways, kids get easier as they get older, no one warns you that the letting go only gets harder. I know that eventually, my kids will be able to do everything for themselves and by themselves, and that crossing the street is just the beginning. But they also know that no matter how tall they are, how smart they become, or how old they get, my hand will always be there for the holding. Just in case.

Crisis Management

SOME PEOPLE CALL IT "THE NEW THIRTY." FOR SOME IT'S A MID-LIFE CRISIS, and for others, it's a mid-life focus. But no matter how you phrase it, there is definitely no denying it. Yes, folks, I am finally forty!

It seems that turning forty has an entirely different dynamic for our generation than it did for our parents'—none of the stigma, but all of the responsibility. When my dad turned forty, most of the presents he received were gag gifts. The only serious-looking gift he got was a fairly conservative red tie with the monogram DOM stitched across the front, which was strange, as his initials are MIG. It wasn't until a few weeks later that my brother discovered a picture of a naked woman hidden inside the tie, and we all realized that DOM actually stood for Dirty Old Man.

Fortieth birthdays now seem less funny and more festive, less mournful and more monumental. Instead of being over the hill, we are reaching a peak, and we recognize it as just one of many in our lives. For me, the hardest thing about turning forty isn't figuring out how to deal with my age, it's figuring out how I got to be this age so quickly.

My life has flown by like summer camp. One summer, when I was thirteen and my brother, Stuart, was eleven, we were at the same overnight camp for eight weeks. Every morning I would walk by his cabin on the way to breakfast and see him and his bunkmates engaged in the same quirky ritual. Since the weeks went by so quickly, Stuart's counselor decided they should acknowledge every single day. So each morning they would stand on their front porch and, with an exaggerated wave, they would proclaim to the world, "HELLO DAY!" And somehow that simple gesture made a big difference.

While I am eager to relish each moment and embrace my age, I admit I'm in a state of denial about the repercussions of getting older. I'm just glad that the pesky veins on my legs, the gray hairs on my head, and the blurred words in my morning newspaper are nothing that can't be easily remedied by a pair of leggings, a trip to the salon, and a strategically hidden magnifying glass in my kitchen.

And even though my eyesight has worsened, my vision has never been clearer when I see my life as a whole.

At forty, I feel mentally sharper, physically stronger, and more self-confident than ever before. (This is true despite the fact that I have a pathetic short-term memory, I dread working out, and I still can't leave the house without getting confirmation from at least one family member that my outfit does not make my butt look big.)

At forty, I understand that being flexible is an asset, not a weakness. I realize that marriage is hard work, that raising children is even harder work, and that I wouldn't trade either for all the M&Ms in the world.

At forty, I can eat chips and dip for dinner without feeling guilty, I will readily admit that I love watching bad reality television more than reading a great book, and I finally have a decent collection of bathing suits that I am not embarrassed to wear in public.

And most important of all, at forty I realize that for all the degrees and plans and hopes and dreams I had when I was in my twenties, there is no way I could have fully anticipated or mapped out the many calculated detours and unexpected forks in the road that have ultimately become my life's journey.

A few months ago, I had the pleasure of speaking with a group of dynamic twenty-somethings about building their résumés and job searching, and someone asked, "Do you believe in making a five-year plan?" I've been thinking about that question ever since, and I finally have an answer.

Yes, I do believe in a five-year plan, and mine is pretty simple: to be forty-five years old, to embrace and celebrate all that comes with it, and to begin each morning by walking out my front door and, with an exaggerated wave, proclaiming to the world, "HELLO DAY!"

ACKNOWLEDGEMENTS

They say it takes a village to publish a book. In my case, it took a team of three very talented and dedicated individuals who could easily run a small country. Heartfelt thanks and gratitude go to my esteemed editor, Allison Gorman, for always shooting from the hip, carefully analyzing every phrase, word, and punctuation mark, and easily trumping every pop culture reference or parenting story with one of her own; my illustrious illustrator, Cindy Procious, for effortlessly translating my somewhat muddled ideas into clever, clear, and creative illustrations on the inside and outside of this book (and for making the minivan just black enough); and my devoted designer, Jane Aylward, for assembling a hundred moving parts into one cohesive unit while being utterly efficient, patient, and flexible along the way. (I just hope one of you will finally tell me what "de-squish" means.) Many thanks also to Jay Taffet and Avi Jorisch for sharing their trade secrets with me and steering me in several right directions, and my friend Lauren Hunt for her brilliant bumper sticker ideas (told you I'd give you credit). And finally, I am eternally indebted to all my family and friends and anyone and everyone who was mentioned in this book for never editing what you said or carefully watching how you acted in my presence for fear it would someday be turned into a column. I'll bet you never bargained it would become a book, too.

Photo by Sergio Plecas

Alison Goldstein Lebovitz is a columnist for *Chattanooga Parent* magazine and the host of *The A List with Alison Lebovitz*, a weekly television interview series that airs on WTCI/PBS in Chattanooga, Tennessee, and statewide on The Tennessee Channel. Alison is also co-founder and president of One Clip at a Time, a nonprofit inspired by the "Paper Clips Project" started in Whitwell, Tennessee. One Clip at a Time promotes student activism and supports service learning in classrooms across the country. A native of Birmingham, Alabama, Alison graduated with honors from Brandeis University with a bachelor's degree in English and American studies, and holds a master's degree in radio/television/film from Northwestern University. Alison and her husband, Alan, live in Chattanooga with their three children, Arthur, Abe, and Levi, and their chocolate Lab, Hershey Bean. Visit her website at www.alisonlebovitz.com.